Hot Topics **1**

CHERYL PAVLIK

THOMSON

HEINLE

Austrialia • Canada • Mexico • Singapore • United Kingdom • United States

HOT TOPICS 1
by *Cheryl Pavlik*

Publisher, Adult and Academic ESL: *James W. Brown*
Senior Acquisitions Editor: *Sherrise Roehr*
Director of Product Development: *Anita Raducanu*
Development Editor: *Sarah Barnicle*
Editorial Assistants: *Katherine Reilly; Bridget McLaughlin; Lindsey Musen*
Director of Product Marketing: *Amy Mabley*
Senior Field Marketing Manager: *Donna Lee Kennedy*
Product Marketing Manager: *Laura Needham*

International Marketing Manager: *Ian Martin*
Senior Production Editor: *Maryellen Killeen*
Senior Print Buyer: *Mary Beth Hennebury*
Photo Researcher: *Melissa Goodrum*
Contributing Writer: *Hilary Grant*
Project Manager: *Tunde A. Dewey*
Compositor: *Parkwood Composition*
Text Printer/Binder: *Transcontinental Printing*
Cover and Interior Designer: *Lori Stuart*

For more information, contact Thomson Heinle, 25 Thomson Place, Boston, MA 02210 USA, or you can visit our Internet site at elt.thomson.com

For permission to use material from this text or product, contact us:
Tel   1-800-730-2214
Fax   1-800-730-2215
Web   www.thomsonrights.com

Library of Congress Control Number
2005928010

ISBN 13: 978-1-4130-0702-2
ISBN 10: 1-4130-0702-3
International Student Edition ISBN: 1-4130-0928-X

BRIEF CONTENTS

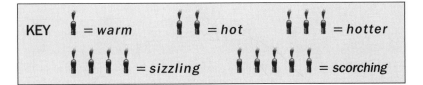

CONTENTS

* In addition to chapter-specific reading and vocabulary skills, each chapter includes exercises to practice the following skills: previewing, predicting, skimming, scanning, fact-finding, analyzing guessing meaning from related words, guessing meaning from context, critical thinking, and discussion questions.

CONTENTS

* In addition to chapter-specific reading and vocabulary skills, each chapter includes exercises to practice the following skills: previewing, predicting, skimming, scanning, fact-finding, analyzing guessing meaning from related words, guessing meaning from context, critical thinking, and discussion questions.

TO THE TEACHER

In the 30 years that I have been in English language training (ELT), I have despaired of the lack of stimulating reading texts, accompanied by activities written specifically to energize and inspire the mature English learner. Why aren't many ESL reading texts sufficient? Although ESL learners may not yet have mastered English syntax, they still have interests beyond the mundane, and they certainly have ample reasoning ability. And while many reading texts are written about subjects of broad appeal, virtually all of them avoid topics that are deemed "too controversial" for the classroom setting. Unfortunately, many of those neglected topics are of great interest and relevance to adult lives. By steering course themes away from controversy, the instructor also steers students away from motivating and stimulating topics.

Hot Topics 1 is different from other reading and discussion texts because it dares to deal with demanding subjects such as *gluttony* and *cultural ideas of beauty*. These topics have not been chosen to shock students, but merely to give them a chance to talk about matters that people discuss every day in their first language. That said, not every topic will be appropriate for every classroom. Some themes such as *intelligence* will probably be acceptable in any classroom. Others such as *Las Vegas* or *Drug Trends* might prove problematic in some teaching situations. To assist, each chapter in the table of contents is rated by the amount of controversy it is likely to cause. Of course, teachers should read the articles in each chapter carefully and decide if their students would feel comfortable having a discussion on a particular topic. Another way to determine which chapters to use in class might be to have students look through the book and then vote on specific topics they are interested in reading and discussing. Even though the chapters at the beginning of each book are generally easier than the chapters at the end, the text has been designed so that chapters can be omitted entirely or covered in a different order.

Series Overview

Hot Topics is a three-level reading discussion series written for inquisitive, mature students of English language learners. Each chapter contains several high-interest readings on a specific controversial and thought-provoking topic.

Reading Selections

Each level of *Hot Topics* consists of 14 chapters. The readings in *Hot Topics* are crafted to present students with challenging reading material including some vocabulary that one might not expect to find in a low-level text. The reason for this is twofold. First, it is almost impossible to deal with these "hot" topics in a meaningful way without more sophisticated vocabulary. Second, and more importantly, it is ineffective to teach reading strategies using materials that provide no challenge. In the same way that one would not use a hammer to push in a thumbtack, readers do not need reading strategies when the meaning of a text is evident. Reading strategies are best learned when one *has to* employ them to aid comprehension.

Each chapter in the book is composed of two parts. Part I will contain two short readings on a topic. These readings are preceded by activities that help students make guesses about the genre, level, and content of the material, activating student schemata or bases of knowledge before reading the text. The readings are followed by extensive exercises that help students thoroughly analyze the content and the structure of the readings.

Part II consists of a single, more challenging reading. Although more difficult, the readings in Part II have direct topical and lexical connection to the readings in Part I. Research shows that the amount of background knowledge one has on a subject directly affects reading comprehension. Therefore, these readings will move the students to an even higher reading level by building on the concepts, information, and vocabulary that they have acquired in Part I. Complete comprehension of the text will not be expected, however. For some students this will prove a difficult task in itself. However, learning to cope with a less than full understanding is an important reading strategy—probably one of the most useful ones that nonnative readers will learn.

Chapter Outline and Teaching Suggestions

PART I

Preview

This section contains prereading questions, photographs, and activities that introduce the topic and some of the vocabulary. This section is best completed as group work or class discussion.

Predict

In this section, students are directed to look at certain features of the text(s) and then make predictions. These predictions include areas such as content, genre, level of difficulty, and reliability of the information.

Read It

This section is generally composed of two readings centered on a particular "hot" topic. In each reading, the topic is approached in a different style, chosen so that students will be able to experience a variety of genres such as newspaper and magazine articles, interviews, pamphlets, charts, and advertisements. Photographs occasionally serve as prompts to assist comprehension, or to stimulate curiosity and conversation about the topics.

Reading Comprehension

The reading comprehension section is composed of three sections.

- **Check Your Predictions**—Students are asked to evaluate their predicting ability.
- **Check the Facts**—Students answer factual questions. This is meant to be fairly simple and the exercise can be completed individually or in groups.
- **Analyze**—This section will include more sophisticated questions that will have students make inferences, as well as analyze and synthesize the information they have read.

Vocabulary Work

Vocabulary Work has two sections.

- **Guess Meaning from Context**—Exercises highlight probable unknown vocabulary words that students should be able to guess using different types of contextual clues. Some of the most common clues students should be looking for include: internal definitions, *restatement* or synonyms that precede or follow the new word, and examples. However, one of the most powerful ways to guess is to use *real world* knowledge. Students must learn to trust their own ability to make educated guesses about meaning based on their own experience.
- **Guess Meaning from Related Words**—This section focuses on words that can be guessed through

morphological analysis. Although morphology is a "context clue," it is so important, that it requires a chapter section of its own. The more students learn to recognize related words, the faster their vocabularies will grow. Students who speak languages such as Spanish—a language that has a large number of cognates or words that look similar to their English counterparts—should also be encouraged to use their native language knowledge as well.

Reading Skills

This section focuses on helpful reading skills and strategies, such as analyzing organization, understanding tone, understanding the author's purpose, and identifying referents and transitional expressions.

Discussion

Questions in this section are designed to encourage class or group discussion. For instructors wishing to follow-up the readings with writing responses, it would be helpful for students to first discuss and then write their individual opinions and/or summarize those of their peers.

PART II

Readings in Part II have been written to be more challenging than those in Part I, so students are asked to read only for the most important ideas. The readings are written so that

- important ideas are stated more than once.
- important ideas are not obscured by difficult vocabulary and high-level structures.
- vocabulary from Part I readings is "built in" or recycled.
- some "new" vocabulary words are forms of words already seen in Part I.

Two activity sections follow the Part II reading. The first consists of questions that will help

students pinpoint the main ideas. The second asks students to make educated guesses about vocabulary they encountered in Part I.

Idea Exchange

Each chapter ends with a comprehensive discussion activity called Idea Exchange. This activity has two steps.

- **Think about Your Ideas**—This section is a structured exercise that helps students clarify their thoughts before they are asked to speak. By filling out charts, answering questions, or putting items in order, students clarify their ideas on the topic.
- **Talk about Your Ideas**—The language in this activity is directly applicable to the discussion questions in the step above.

CNN® Video Activities

The CNN video news clip activities at the back of the student text are thematically related to each chapter. Activities are designed to recycle themes and vocabulary from each chapter, and to encourage further class discussion and written responses.

A Word on Methodology and Classroom Management

Class Work, Group Work, Pair Work, and Individual Work

One of the most basic questions a teacher must decide before beginning an activity is whether it is best done as class work, group work, or individual work. Each has its place in the language classroom. For some activities, the answer is obvious. Reading should always be an individual activity. Reading aloud to the class can be pronunciation practice for the reader or listening practice for the listeners, but it is not reading for comprehension.

On the other hand, many activities in this text can be done successfully in pairs, groups, or with the entire class working together. If possible, a mix of individual, pair, group, and class work is probably best. For example, two students may work together and then share their work with a larger group that then shares its ideas with the entire class.

Some rules of thumb are:

• Pair work is often most successful in activities that have one right answer. Pairs should be able to check their answers or at least share them with the class.

• Groups work best when one group member records the discussion, so that the group can then report to the class. In this way, everyone gets the maximum benefit.

• Think of yourself as the manager of a whole class activity rather than the focal point. Make sure that students talk to each other, not just to you. For example, you might appoint yourself secretary and write students' ideas on the board as they are talking.

Error Correction

Language errors are bound to occur in discussions at this level. However, the purpose of the discussions in this text is fluency not accuracy. Therefore, errors should not be dealt with unless they make comprehension difficult or impossible. Make unobtrusive notes about persistent errors that you want to deal with later. In those cases where it is difficult to understand what a student is trying to say, first give the student a chance to clarify. If they cannot do this, restate what you think they are trying to say.

Dictionaries

Frequent dictionary use makes reading a slow, laborious affair. Students should be taught first to try to guess the meaning of a word using context and word form clues before they resort to a dictionary. In addition, although a good learner's English-English dictionary is helpful, bilingual dictionaries should be discouraged, as they are often inaccurate. Students should use a dictionary that supplies simple and clear definitions, context sentences, and synonyms. We recommend *Heinle's Newbury House Dictionary with CD-ROM, 3rd Edition.*

We would like to thank the following reviewers for their ideas and helpful suggestions regarding the Hot Topics series:

Chiou-Lan Chern
National Taiwan Normal University, Taipei, Taiwan

C.J. Dalton
Institution Verbatim English, Belo Horizante, Brazil

Judith Finkelstein
Reseda Community Adult School, Reseda, CA, United States

Patricia Brenner
University of Washington, Seattle, WA, United States

Renee Klosz
Lindsey Hopkins Technical Education Center, Miami, FL, United States

Eric Rosenbaum
BEGIN Managed Programs, New York, NY, United States

Finally, thanks to all instructors who, by selecting the *Hot Topics* series, recognize that ESL students are mature learners who have the right to read about unconventional and provocative topics. By offering your students challenging reading topics that encourage curiosity and debate, their ideas and opinions will become essential and fruitful parts of their classroom experience.

CHERYL PAVLIK

PHOTO CREDITS

CHAPTER 1

Pampered Pets: Love me? Love my dog!

parrot

rat

cat

dog

hamster

rabbit

pig

fish

PREVIEW

Discuss the answers to these questions.

1. Which of these animals are good pets?
2. Do people in your country keep pets? If so, what kind?
3. Why do people keep pets?

1

PART I

Predict

A. Quickly skim the two articles. Circle the answers.

Which article . . .

1. is an advertisement?

   Reading 1   Reading 2   Readings 1 & 2

2. talks about an idea in general?

   Reading 1   Reading 2   Readings 1 & 2

3. has information from people who disagree?

   Reading 1   Reading 2   Readings 1 & 2

4. uses quotes from pet owners?

   Reading 1   Reading 2   Readings 1 & 2

B. Write a question that you think each article will answer.

Reading 1: _____

Reading 2: _____

Read It

Read the articles. Look for the answers to your questions.

 READING 1   ### New Restaurant with That Special Dog in Mind

Do you want to get your dog a special birthday present? If you live in Chicago, you can take Spike or Fifi out to dinner at the Pet Café. It has tables for the humans and eating stands for the dogs. A meal costs less than four dollars. For that price, your dog gets an entrée, a fortune dog biscuit (the canine version of a fortune cookie), and a bowl of peanut-butter flavored ice cream. You, the owner, on the other hand, are only offered candy.

You may think a restaurant for dogs is strange. However, restaurant owner Vera Carter does not. She says, "People want to return the loyalty and love their animals give them. For a dog, the best way to do that is to give them good food."

Carl Gregory, a pet-industry expert agrees. He says Americans are not just buying food; they are spending millions of dollars on toys, beds, classes, and even clothing for their pets. In fact, today Americans spend twice as much on their pets as they did in 1994. In that year, they spent about 17 million dollars. In 2004, they spent more than 34 million dollars.

For these reasons, many different types of businesses are offering services to pet owners. Some hotels now rent pet-friendly rooms. Some even have room service for dogs. Mail-order companies offering steak for dogs have become more popular. There are also many bakeries selling pet treats in addition to pies and cakes for people. More and more restaurants are adding food for pets to their menus. However, there aren't many sit-down pet restaurants like the Pet Café.

Some people don't like the idea of a restaurant for dogs. As Web blogger Jack Simpson says, "Dog restaurants are absurd." Dog owner Sherry Evans doesn't agree. She went to the Pet Café with her dog, Lulu. "No, it's not ridiculous," she says. "Everyone has to feel needed. Lulu is my sweet, precious baby."

 READING 2   Camp Hideaway

You want to take a vacation, but you are worried about your pet. Who will take care of Fluffy, Roger, or Princess? Now you can leave town with confidence. Just take your pet to Camp Hideaway—an all-season camp for your favorite animal. Camp Hideaway is a high-class place. It's just like summer camp for children! Campers have pool time, and they also have special play times. Camp Hideaway has indoor heated dog runs and a big outdoor area for playful, social dogs.

In some ways, it's better than summer camps children enjoy.

Camp Hideaway has television. Sparky can go to the doggie TV room, sit on the couch, and watch television with his friends. Individual personalities are also respected. Is your pet shy? There is a separate exercise area for dogs or cats that like to be alone. Like your dog, your cat won't be bored either. She will have a private room with windows. She can look outside and see birds and fish. She will also have lots of toys to play with. To help all the animals relax, there is classical music 24 hours a day. Camp Hideaway's counselors also follow your pet's daily schedule. If you want, you can bring in your pet's own food, treats, toys, and bed. Your little camper will be so happy that he may never want to go home!

Reading Comprehension

Check Your Predictions

1. Look back at questions 1–4 in the Predict section. How correct were your predictions?

Prediction	Incorrect	Correct
1		
2		
3		
4		

2. If you found the answers to your questions, what were they?

Reading 1: _____

Reading 2: _____

Check the Facts

Check (✓) the questions you can answer after reading once. Then go back and look for the answer you are unsure of.

READING 1

A. Read the statements and write *true* (T) or *false* (F). Go back to Reading 1 and look for the answers you are unsure of.

_____ 1. People can eat at the Pet Café.

_____ 2. Dogs eat at tables at the Pet Café.

_____ 3. Americans are spending less money on pets than they did before.

_____ 4. Some hotels allow pets to stay.

_____ 5. Everyone thinks that pet restaurants are a good idea.

_____ 6. There are many pet restaurants in the United States.

_____ 7. Some regular restaurants sell food for pets.

B. Answer the questions.

1. The writer quotes several people. What is each person's position?

   Vera Carter _____

   Carl Gregory _____

   Jack Simpson _____

   Sherry Evans _____

2. What unusual services do each of these types of businesses offer to pets?

   hotels: _____ and _____

   restaurants: _____

   bakeries: _____

A. Read the statements and write *true* **(T) or** *false* **(F). Go back to Reading 2 and look for the answers you are unsure of.**

_____ 1. Camp Hideaway is for only for pets.

_____ 2. Camp Hideaway has services for cats, dogs, birds, and fish.

_____ 3. The camp is only for social animals.

_____ 4. Cats stay in rooms with birds and fish.

_____ 5. Not all pets follow the same daily schedule at the camp.

_____ 6. Pet owners must bring their pet's own food and bed.

B. Answer the questions.

1. How is Camp Hideaway like a camp for children?

    _____

    _____

2. What special things does Camp Hideaway have for cats? For dogs?

    _____

    _____

Analyze

Answer these questions. Give reasons for your answers.

1. Do you think Carl Gregory has a pet?
2. Do some people travel with their pets?
3. Do you think Sherry Evans has children?
4. Is Camp Hideaway probably more expensive than dog pounds or kennels?
5. What do the names Fifi, Sparky, Fluffy, Roger, and Princess refer to? Why did the writer use them?

Vocabulary Work

Guess Meaning from Context: Using World Knowledge

You can use your world knowledge to guess the meaning of a word. For example, you may not know the meaning of entrée *in Reading 1. However, you might think like this:*

> I know about restaurants and menus. I know that a meal in a restaurant is often a main dish and a dessert. Peanut-butter ice cream is a dessert. Therefore, entrée is probably the main dish.

Often you can combine world knowledge with other clues. If you don't understand room service, *you might think like this:*

> I know room service is something in a hotel. In addition, I understand the word room. Service looks like serve. I know people serve you in a restaurant. I also know that in a hotel people will bring food to your room. So, maybe room service is bringing food to your room.

When you guess the meaning of a word, you should use your knowledge of the world. What real-world experiences can help you guess the meaning of these words?

eating stands   _____

pet treats   _____

dog runs   _____

Understanding Summaries

Writers often introduce a quote with a summary of the speaker's words. If you understand the summary, you do not have to understand all the words in the quote.

A. Find two summaries in the paragraph below. Do you understand the <u>underlined</u> words? Does it matter?

Some people don't like the idea of a restaurant for dogs. As Web blogger Jack Simpson says, "Dog restaurants are <u>absurd</u>." Dog owner Sherry Evans doesn't agree. She went to the Pet Café with her dog, Lulu. "No, it's not <u>ridiculous</u>," she says. "Everyone has to feel needed. Lulu is my <u>sweet, precious</u> baby."

B. Sometimes an example helps to guess the meaning of an unknown word. What may help you to guess the meaning of <u>twice</u> in the third paragraph of Reading 1?

Guess Meaning from Related Words

When two or more descriptive words before a noun act as one idea, they are connected with a hyphen. For example, compare the phrase <u>playful, social dogs</u> with <u>high-class place</u>. <u>Playful</u> and <u>social</u> are not hyphenated. They refer to two different ideas. The dogs are <u>playful</u>, and they are <u>social</u>. However, <u>high-class</u> refers to one idea. Therefore, these two words are hyphenated.

Find the hyphenated descriptive words in Reading 1. Write a meaning for each phrase.

Phrase	Meaning
_____	_____
_____	_____
_____	_____
_____	_____
_____	_____

Reading Skills

Identifying the Author's Purpose

1. Which article informs readers? What information does the author want the readers to know?

2. Which article persuades readers? What does the author want readers to do?

3. Look at Reading 1.

    a. How does the author use quotes?

    b. Do you know the author's opinion?

4. Look at Reading 2.

    a. How does the author use punctuation?

    b. What positive words can you find?

    c. Do you know the author's opinion? How?

Discussion

1. Would you take your dog to a restaurant?

2. Would you go to a restaurant that served animals?

3. Would you stay in a hotel that allowed animals?

4. What should people with pets do when they go on vacation?

PART II

This reading is more difficult than the articles in Part I. Read it for the main ideas. Do not worry if you cannot understand everything.

Read to find the answers to these questions.

1. What are *clones*?
2. What does the company Genetic Savings and Clone do?
3. What guarantee does the company give?
4. Do all pet owners want to clone their pets? Why or why not?

 READING Life after Death?

Kittens Tabouli and Baba Ganoush look alike, but they aren't twins. They're clones. Feline clones are exact genetic copies of another cat. They were created in a laboratory by a company called Genetic Savings and Clone. The company expects to make a lot of money cloning pets after they die. Lou Hawthorne, the president of the company, says, "It's a multibillion-dollar business waiting to happen." Hawthorne's company already has a list of people who want cloned cats. They will each pay $50,000. Dogs will cost more. "We guarantee that the clone will be healthy and that it will look very much like the original animal," Hawthorne says.

One woman has ordered a clone of her late cat. "I made the decision to clone him before he died. Then I had hope that I might share a part of him again," Marsha Brooks says. For many people, losing a beloved pet is very upsetting. It can be like losing a member of the family. But even some pet lovers say that cloning seems absurd. However, this cat owner doesn't agree. She wants her cat back. "He was more intelligent than most of the people I know," she said. "And I can't wait to meet the clone!"

But while one woman waits for a clone, others are looking for new pets. Karen and Michael Lawrence decided to spend $50 instead of $50,000. When their cat, Marshall, died, they went to the animal shelter. "You know, there are a lot of great cats and dogs who don't have homes." said Karen.

Vocabulary Work

Guess Meaning from Context

1. Can you guess the meanings of these words? What clues did you use?

   a. genetic _____

   b. multibillion-dollar _____

   c. guarantee _____

   d. beloved _____

   e. animal shelter _____

2. How do the meanings of the underlined words differ in this reading from the meanings that you know?

   a. losing a pet is very upsetting

   b. her late cat

Reading Skills

Analyzing Quotations

Look back at the reading and underline the quotations.

	Name of the person quoted	For or against cloning?
1.	_____	_____
2.	_____	_____
3.	_____	_____

Idea Exchange

Think about Your Ideas

Answer this questionnaire.

	I think that's OK.	I'm not sure if that's OK.	I don't think that's OK.
People buy their pets special food.			
People cook food for their pets.			
People let their pets live in their houses.			
People let their pets sleep in their rooms.			
People let their pets sleep on their beds.			
People buy their pets toys.			
People take their pets to animal doctors.			
People give their pets vitamins or medicine.			
People send their dogs to training classes.			
People take their pets to animal psychologists.			

Talk about Your Ideas

Think about people you know who have pets. Do you agree with the way they treat them? Why or why not?

For CNN video activities about pampered pet services, turn to page 169.

CHAPTER 2

Silly Sports: Can you really call this a sport?

billiards

wrestling

ballroom dancing

autoracing

synchronized swimming

cheerleading

PREVIEW

Discuss the answer to this question.

Which of these activities are sports? Give reasons for your opinions.

13

PART I

Predict

A. Quickly skim the two articles. Circle the answers.

Which article . . .

1. gives someone's opinion?

   Reading 1   Reading 2   Readings 1 & 2

2. describes a sport?

   Reading 1   Reading 2   Readings 1 & 2

3. begins with an event in the past?

   Reading 1   Reading 2   Readings 1 & 2

4. mostly talks about events in the present tense?

   Reading 1   Reading 2   Readings 1 & 2

B. Write a question that you think each article will answer.

Reading 1: _____

Reading 2: _____

Read It

Read the articles. Look for the answers to your questions.

 (READING 1)   Extreme Ironing

What activities are sports? Running and football? Sure. Synchronized swimming? Probably. Ballroom dancing? Maybe. Playing cards? Probably not. Gardening? Definitely not. Most people believe that sports must combine physical activity and competition. If we use this definition, then extreme ironing is a sport.

What is *extreme ironing*? Extreme ironing is pressing clothes in very difficult places. Ironists must carry their irons, ironing boards, and wrinkled laundry with them to the competition site. Some ironists take electric generators. Others heat their irons on gas stoves. The competitors get more points for the difficulty of the location. However, the quality of the ironing is important, too. Each item must be well pressed.

Extreme ironists compete in some amazing places. Contestants iron while they are climbing rocks, climbing mountains, and climbing trees. They iron in canoes, on the backs of cows, and even underwater. One team ironed while on a kayak in the Atlantic Ocean.

This sport is not a joke. Teams from 30 countries competed in the first world championships in Germany in 2002. Phil Shaw is the inventor of extreme ironing. He says that there are about 1,500 ironists worldwide. Some teams have corporate sponsors. The German corporation Rowenta, an iron maker, pays for Shaw's team. The goal of extreme ironists is to have their sport included in the Olympics. Maybe then they can start using their real names. At the moment, contestants use names such as Steam, Cool Silk, and Iron Man. Why? Shaw admits, "Most competitors don't want people to know that they are ironists."

 READING 2

Eating to Live

KENNEBUNK, MAINE—
Sonya Thomas of Alexandria, Virginia, finished 38 lobsters in 12 minutes and won the World Lobster-Eating Contest on Saturday. She ate a total of 4.39 kilograms of lobster meat. Sonya won $500 and a trophy.

Sonya has a lot of trophies. She is a professional *gurgitator*— she eats for a living. The

(Continued on page 16)

International Federation of Competitive Eating (IFOCE) says that Thomas is the best gurgitator in the United States. In fact, a few days before the lobster competition, she won a bean-eating competition. She ate 4 kilos of beans in 2 minutes and 47 seconds. She also holds the record for hard-boiled eggs (65 in 6 minutes) and tacos (43 in 11 minutes). Sonya is the only American who could possibly beat Japanese gurgitator Takeru Kobayashi. He is ranked number one in the world. He is the champion in eating hot dogs, rice balls, and cow brains.

You might think that professional eaters must look like sumo wrestlers. They don't. In fact, most of them are not fat at all. Kobayashi weighs only 50 kilograms and Sonya Thomas just 45. What is their secret? Metal buckets, perhaps.

Professional eating is serious business. Gurgitators travel from one championship to another just like golfers and tennis players. First, there is the chicken-wing competition, then the matzo-ball competition, followed by the pickle-eating championship, and so on. The most important competition is Nathan's Hot-Dog Eating Contest. It is held in New York every July. It is the Olympics of a sport that will *never* be in the Olympics.

Reading Comprehension

Check Your Predictions

1. Look back at questions 1–4 in the Predict section. How correct were your predictions?

Prediction	Correct	Incorrect
1		
2		
3		
4		

2. If you found the answers to your questions, what were they?

Reading 1: _____

Reading 2: _____

Check the Facts

A. Read the statements and write *true* (T) or *false* (F). Go back to Reading 1 and look for the answers you are unsure of.

_____ 1. The writer believes that sports must be competitive.

_____ 2. The writer believes that sports must be dangerous.

_____ 3. Extreme ironing is a very old sport.

_____ 4. Extreme ironists almost always compete outside.

_____ 5. Some companies sponsor extreme ironing teams.

_____ 6. Extreme ironists don't like people to know their names.

B. Answer the questions.

1. Check (✓) the items that ironists must carry with them.

_____ iron

_____ ironing board

_____ electric generator

_____ clothes

_____ laundry basket

_____ gas stove

_____ food

2. What do ironists get points for?

a. how much laundry they iron

b. how fast they iron

c. how well they iron

d. how long they iron

3. What else do they get points for?

a. when they iron

b. where they iron

c. what they iron

d. why they iron

A. Read the statements and write *true* (T) or *false* (F). Go back to Reading 2 and look for the answers you are unsure of.

_____ 1. Sonya Thomas ate 12 lobsters in 38 minutes.

_____ 2. Competitive eating is Sonya's job.

_____ 3. Sonya is a member of the IFOCE.

_____ 4. Sonya is the best professional eater in the world.

_____ 5. Professional eaters are fat.

_____ 6. Professional eaters play golf and tennis.

_____ 7. The most important competition is a hot-dog eating contest.

B. Answer the questions.

1. What two things are most important in competitive eating contest?

   a. speed

   b. style

   c. amount

   d. taste

2. Name three different eating contests.

   _____

   _____

   _____

Analyze

1. Would the writer of Reading 1 think that professional eating is a sport?

2. Sometimes writers let their readers infer or guess part of their meaning. What connection does the writer want the reader to make in the quote below?

   You might think that professional eaters must look like sumo wrestlers. They don't . . . What is their secret? Metal buckets perhaps.

Vocabulary Work

Guess Meaning from Context

Sometimes you can guess the meaning of a word in a list by looking at the other words in the list. You may not know the meaning of wrinkled laundry. *How can the list help you guess what it is?*

> Ironists must carry their irons, ironing boards, and wrinkled laundry with them to the competition site.

Sometimes you can only guess the category of the word. What category do the underlined words belong to?

> First, there is the <u>chicken-wing</u> competition, then the <u>matzo-ball</u> competition, followed by the <u>pickle</u>-eating championship, and so on.

Use the context to guess the approximate meanings of the <u>underlined</u> words.

1. Some take <u>electric generators</u>. Others heat their irons on <u>gas stoves</u>.

2. However, the quality of the ironing is important, too. Each item must be <u>well pressed</u>.

3. Some teams have corporate <u>sponsors</u>. The German corporation Rowenta, an iron maker, pays for Shaw's team.

4. One team ironed while on a <u>kayak</u> in the Atlantic Ocean.

Guess Meaning from Related Words

1. The following words are in the readings. Find other words that are related to them.

   Reading 1

   compete   _____

                                 _____

   corporation   _____

   champion   _____

   Reading 2

   competition   _____

   champion   _____

2. How do you know if a word is a verb, noun, adjective, or adverb?

   • *Verbs usually have subjects. They also often have endings such as -ed, -ing, or -s.*
   • *Nouns often are preceded by* <u>a</u>, <u>an</u> *or* <u>the</u>. *They sometimes have -s at the end.*
   • *Adjectives often come before nouns or after the verb* be.
   • *Adverbs often end in -ly.*

   Work in pairs. Draw a chart like this one in your notebook. Put the words from Exercise 1 above in the correct columns.

Noun (person)	Noun (thing)	Verb	Adjective	Adverb

3. Look at these compounds nouns. What do they mean? Complete the sentences.

    a. An *ironing board* is something that you use to _____.

    b. An *electric generator* is something that _____.

    c. A *gas stove* is something that _____.

    d. *Underwater* means _____.

    e. *Ballroom dancing* is a kind of _____.

    f. *Synchronized swimming* is a kind of _____.

Reading Skills

Finding Main Ideas and Supporting Details

Every paragraph in a reading should have a main idea. The writer often starts the paragraph with the main idea. The writer then uses details to explain the main idea.

Write the main ideas of each paragraph in Reading 1. Then add one detail from each paragraph.

Paragraph 1   Main Idea _____

                Detail _____

Paragraph 2   Main Idea _____

                Detail _____

Paragraph 3   Main Idea _____

                Detail _____

Paragraph 4   Main Idea _____

                Detail _____

Discussion

1. What do you think of extreme ironing and professional eating? Are they sports? Would you participate in them?

2. Are there any other sports that you think are silly?

PART II

Read the next article to find the answers to these questions.

1. According to the writer, which of these activities are sports?

   figure skating   *golf*   *gymnastics*   *baseball*

2. How did he make his decision?
3. Do all athletes participate in sports?
4. Is everyone who participates in a sport an athlete?

 READING

What Makes a Sport?

What is a sport? In my opinion, there are some activities that are definitely sports: baseball, football, basketball, hockey, golf, and bowling. And there are some activities that are definitely **not** sports: cheerleading, dance, figure skating, and gymnastics.

How did I decide? An activity is not a sport if a judge or a group of judges chooses the winner. The competition itself should decide the result. Judges decide the winners of figure skating, cheerleading, dance, and gymnastics competitions. Therefore, none of them are sports.

In the non-sports listed, judges determine the winners based on their opinions. Judges are human and many things can influence them. Maybe they think one competitor wins too often or not enough. Perhaps they don't like one of the contestants. Perhaps they just prefer one competitor's music or their clothes. The point is that we can never be certain that the winner was really the best.

Of course, you might say that every sport has judges. Umpires in baseball and referees in basketball make decisions, too. However, one bad decision by an official doesn't decide the winner of these games. The competition does.

According to my definition, activities like bowling, Ping-Pong, and even curling are sports. The person or team that has more points or finishes first wins. The opinion of a judge is not necessary.

There is one more important point. You can be an athlete and not participate in a sport. Cheerleaders, dancers, gymnasts, and figure skaters are incredible athletes. Their activities require a lot of athleticism, strength, and flexibility. They are athletes, but they do not participate in sports. They participate in athletic competitions. In addition, you can participate in a sport and not be an athlete. Bowlers and golfers do not have to be great athletes. They are people with a specific skill, but they are not athletes.

There is one exception to my definition. NASCAR is not a sport. It is simply entertainment. And, in my opinion, it's not even good entertainment.

Adapted with permission from an article by Brian Grossman, published in *Technician*, an online publication of North Carolina State University

Vocabulary Work

Guess Meaning from Context

Match the words and their meanings. What clues did you use?

1. result
2. determine
3. influence
4. umpires/referees
5. athleticism
6. curling
7. participate

a. people who make sure that competitors follow the rules
b. physical ability
c. decision
d. take part in
e. affect
f. decide
g. a game

Reading Skills

Understanding the Writer's Tone

When you read, it is important to understand the writer's tone. Is the article objective? In other words, does it simply give facts? Does it give both sides of a question?

1. Is this reading objective? Why or why not?
2. Identify some points that readers might not agree with.

Idea Exchange

Think about Your Ideas

Finish these sentences in all the ways that are true for you.

1. A sport must be _____.

competitive	difficult	athletic
serious	skillful	exciting

2. A sport must have _____.

rules	competitors	a clear winner
judges	a time limit	fans

Talk about Your Ideas

1. Do you agree with the following definition of a sport? Why or why not?

   > A human activity that is competitive, has a definite result, requires physical activity and/or physical skill.

2. Would the writer of Reading 3 agree with this definition? Why or why not?

For CNN video activities on the sport of eating, turn to page 170.

CHAPTER 3

Modern Marriage:

Until death do us part?

PREVIEW

Discuss the answers to these questions.

1. What is the divorce rate in your country?
   a. Fifty percent or higher.
   b. Less than 50 percent.
   c. I'm not sure, but I think it's low.
   d. I'm not sure, but I think it's high.
2. What do you think is the main reason people get divorced?
   a. They fall in love with other people.
   b. They disagree about money.
   c. They have problems with their children.
   d. They get married too young.

3. How old are most men and women when they get married in your country?

Men	Women
a. 20–25	a. 20–25
b. 25–30	b. 25–30
c. 31–35	c. 31–35
d. over 35	d. over 35

PART I

Predict

A. Quickly skim the two articles. Answer the questions.

Which article . . .

1. contains statistics?

   Reading 1   Reading 2   Readings 1 & 2

2. talks about scientific research?

   Reading 1   Reading 2   Readings 1 & 2

3. gives advice?

   Reading 1   Reading 2   Readings 1 & 2

4. talks about divorce?

   Reading 1   Reading 2   Readings 1 & 2

B. Write a question that you think each article will answer.

Reading 1: _____

Reading 2: _____

Read It

Read the articles. Look for the answers to your questions.

READING 1

Dear Advisor: Should She Propose?

Dear Advisor,

My boyfriend and I just celebrated three years together. I want to ask him to marry me. My friends say I shouldn't. They say that only desperate women propose marriage. Are they right?

Nervous in New Jersey

Dear Nervous,

Your friends are not right. Today it is fine for women to propose to men. Monica did it on *Friends*. Miranda did it on *Sex and the City*. In real life, actress Halle Berry did it, too.

In 2003, the Korbel Champagne Company conducted a survey. They asked, "Should women ask men to marry them?" Sixty-seven percent of Americans said yes. The survey asked women, "Would you propose to a man?" Almost 50 percent of the women said they would. They also asked men, "Would you accept?" Almost 80 percent said yes. Thirty-one percent of women know a woman who has proposed to a man.

Experts generally agree. Dr. Linda O'Connor has a radio talk show about love and marriage. O'Connor says that women who propose are usually educated and self-confident. In addition, their boyfriends usually like strong women. However, advice columnist Susan Fine argues that even women with a lot of self-confidence may need some help with their proposals. Here is her advice. First, the proposal should not be a surprise. The relationship should be serious. She also advises women to do two more things. They should write out the proposal and practice it before they ask for their boyfriends' hands in marriage.

How would Susan Fine answer you? If you and your boyfriend are happy, do not pay attention to your friends. And don't invite them to the wedding.

—The Advisor

 Divorce: A Fifty-Fifty Chance?

Divorce is a growing problem in the United States and many other developed countries. Although thousands and thousands of happy couples get married every year, more than 50 percent of them get divorced. Two researchers at the University of Washington studied marriage and divorce. They learned a lot from their research. With this information, they created a mathematical formula that predicts divorce. Mathematician James Murray and psychologist John Gottman agree that their predictions are correct almost all of the time.

How do they do it?

A husband and wife talk about a difficult subject for 15 minutes. The researchers videotape them. In addition, they record physical information such as heart rate. Then the researchers listen to the conversation. They watch the body language and look at the facial reactions. After that, they give the couple positive and negative points.

For example, the couple might talk about mothers-in-law. If the husband says, "Your mother is a lot of trouble," the couple gets two negative points. If the wife rolls her eyes, they get two more negative points. However, if the husband says, "Your mother is a lot of trouble, but sometimes she's funny," then the couple gets one positive point. If he smiles, they get another one.

In the end, the researchers add up the points. A good marriage has five more positive points than negative points. However, the researchers say that a bad score is not necessarily the end of a marriage. Marriages with bad scores can survive. They hope that couples will use the information from the study to learn to communicate. However, not everyone believes that mathematics can stop divorce. A professor of psychology at New York University says that it is "absolutely impossible" to use mathematics to help a marriage. The scientists disagree. They have studied this problem for 16 years. In that time, they have studied more than 700 couples. Their predictions are 94 percent accurate. It seems necessary for the survival of marriage that we listen to them.

Reading Comprehension

Check Your Predictions

1. Look back at questions 1–4 in the Predict section. How correct were your predictions?

Prediction	Not correct	Correct
1		
2		
3		
4		

2. If you found the answers to your questions, what were they?

Reading 1: _____

Reading 2: _____

Check the Facts

READING 1

A. **Read the statements and write *true* (T) or *false* (F). Go back to Reading 1 and look for the answers you are unsure of.**

_____ 1. Susan Fine is on the radio.

_____ 2. "Nervous in New Jersey" wrote to Susan Fine.

_____ 3. "Nervous in New Jersey" is a man.

_____ 4. "Nervous in New Jersey" wants to get married.

_____ 5. In 2003 most women said that only men should propose.

_____ 6. Dr. Linda O'Connor is a divorce lawyer.

_____ 7. The Advisor told "Nervous in New Jersey" to propose to her boyfriend.

B. Answer the questions.

1. According to O'Connor, which adjectives describe women who propose to men?

funny *educated* *desperate* *strong*
self-confident *nervous* *weak*

2. What two suggestions does Susan Fine make?

_____

_____

READING 2

A. Read the statements and write *true* (T) or *false* (F). Go back to Reading 2 and look for the answers you are unsure of.

_____ 1. Most married couples get divorced.

_____ 2. There is a mathematical formula that predicts who should get married.

_____ 3. A mathematician worked with a sociologist.

_____ 4. For their study, the researchers videotaped couples.

_____ 5. The couples took a written test.

_____ 6. The researchers gave each couple positive and negative points.

_____ 7. If the score is bad, the couple has to get divorced.

_____ 8. The formula predicts incorrectly 6 percent of the time.

B. Answer the questions.

1. What three things do the researchers look at?

_____

_____

_____

2. Find two examples of *body language* or *facial reactions* in the reading.

_____

_____

Analyze

1. Which one of these women are real? How do you know?
   - Monica
   - Miranda
   - Halle Berry
2. Why do you think Korbel Champagne Company did a survey about marriage?

Vocabulary Work

Guess Meaning from Context

A. Match the words from Readings 1 and 2 with their meanings.

1. desperate	a. ask to marry
2. propose	b. sure of oneself
3. self-confident	c. hopeless
4. research	d. continue to live
5. survive	e. study

B. What is the meaning of the underlined words or phrases from the readings?
   1. Today it is fine for women . . .
   2. . . . physical information such as . . .

Guess Meaning from Related Words

1. The following words are in the readings. Find other words that are related to them.

   Reading 1
   propose   _____
   self-confident   _____
   advice   _____
   column   _____

Reading 2

married   _____

mathematical   _____

predicts   _____

necessary   _____

psychology   _____

agree   _____

2. Work in pairs. Draw a chart like this one in your notebook. Put the words from Exercise 1 in the correct columns. Compare your work with another pair when you are done.

Noun (person)	Noun (thing)	Verb	Adjective	Adverb
	proposal	proposal		

Reading Skills

Understanding Transition Words and Phrases

Many transition words and phrases are used in English. Writers use transition words and phrases to connect ideas. These words and phrases may connect ideas from one sentence to another. They may also connect ideas within the same sentence. Some transition words and phrases add ideas together:

> *He drank the soda **and** ate all the ice cream.*

Some transition words and phrases put actions in time order:

> **First,** *take two eggs.* **Then** *break them in a bowl.*

What do the underlined transition words and phrases from the readings do?

1. <u>In addition</u>, their boyfriends usually like strong women.
2. She <u>also</u> advises women to do two more things.
3. <u>Then</u> the researchers listen to the conversation.
4. <u>After that</u>, they give the couple positive points and negative points.
5. <u>In the end</u>, the researchers add up the points.

Discussion

1. Do you think it is OK for women to propose to men? Why or why not?
2. How important is communication in marriage?
3. Do you think mathematics can predict divorces?

PART II

Read the next article to find the answers to these questions.

1. What two countries does the writer talk about?
2. What is each government doing about marriage?
3. The two government programs try to help different groups. What are the two groups?
4. How do people in each country feel about the programs?

 **READING**

The Government Department of Dating and Marriage?

Many single people need help finding husbands or wives. Some people hire matchmakers. Others use computer dating services on the Internet. Now, at least two governments want to help their citizens tie the knot.

One of them is the United States government. The government in Washington gives each of the 50 states money to encourage marriage. The states are using it to persuade people that marriage is good. Some states are also offering classes on marriage. The government says that the future of the United States depends on strong families. However, its programs are not for all families. They are for one special group—the poor. They want to tell low-income people about the benefits of marriage. Some government officials argue that women with children should have husbands. If they have husbands, they will not need money from the government. Their husbands will work to earn money for their families. Some people are against government programs that promote marriage. They say that marriage is a private decision. They are also afraid that poor women might think they have to get married.

The American government is not the only one that is interested in marriage. The government of the tiny island nation of Singapore is spending money on marriage, too. Why is the government in Singapore interested in marriage? The government has noticed that women with college degrees often do not get married. Government officials think it is important for them to get married, so they have started a government dating service. The Social Development Unit (SDU) began in 1984. It organizes parties and trips for single people. It also teaches single people about marriage. The SDU says that 50,000 Singaporeans have met and married through this service.

And what do young Singaporeans think of the government dating services? Some of them are happy with it. Ms. Ralls-Tan says that the SDU helped her get married. She and her husband married two years ago. Today they have a six-month-old child. Others just laugh at it. "Single, desperate, and ugly," says a young woman at a local bar. Another says, "We're adults. And the government is not our parent."

Vocabulary Work

Guess Meaning from Context

Guess the meaning of these words and phrases from Reading 3. What clues did you use?

Clues: a. It looked like a word I knew.

             b. I used world knowledge.

             c. There was a definition in the reading.

             d. There was an example in the reading.

1. matchmakers _____

2. computer dating service _____

3. promote _____

4. organize _____

Reading Skills

Identifying Referents

What does each <u>underlined</u> word or phrase from Reading 3 refer to?

The government says that the future of the United States depends on strong families. However, <u>its</u> programs are not for all families.
                                1

<u>They</u> are for one special group—the poor. Some government officials
 2
argue that women with children should have husbands. If <u>they</u> have
                                    3
husbands, they will not need money from the government. Some people are against government programs that advertise marriage. <u>They</u> say
                                     4
that marriage is a private decision. <u>They</u> are also afraid that poor
                         5
women might think <u>they</u> have to get married.
                 6

1. _____   4. _____

2. _____   5. _____

3. _____   6. _____

Idea Exchange

Think about Your Ideas

1. How important is marriage for the happiness and future of each group?

	Not very important	Somewhat important	Very important	Extremely important
Men				
Women				
Children				
Society				

2. In your opinion, which are the five most important elements for a successful marriage?

_____ agreement on how to raise children

_____ agreement on money issues

_____ approval from family members

_____ fidelity

_____ open communication

_____ one decision maker

_____ same culture

_____ same religion

_____ satisfactory sexual relationship

_____ shared values

_____ similar level of education

_____ similar personalities

Talk about Your Ideas

Discuss these three points.

1. The government should make it difficult to get married. Every couple should have to pass a course about marriage before they get a marriage license.
2. Governments should use taxes to encourage marriage and discourage divorce. Married couples should pay fewer taxes than single people. Divorced couples should pay a divorce penalty tax.
3. Marriage is a personal decision. The government should not try to control it.

For CNN video activities about marriage and divorce, turn to page 171.

CHAPTER 4

SHOPPING: THE NEW DRUG OF CHOICE

PREVIEW

Answer the questions. Then talk about your answers.

1. How often do you go shopping (not for food)?

   a. Two or three times a week.   c. Twice a month.

   b. Once a week.   d. Once a month or less.

2. How often do you spend money when you go shopping?

   a. Almost always.   c. Sometimes.

   b. Very often.   d. Rarely.

3. How often do you shop in malls?

   a. Almost always.   c. Sometimes.

   b. Very often.   d. Rarely.

4. What's the best thing about indoor malls?

a. There are lots of stores.

b. You don't have to think about the weather.

c. There are a lot of people.

d. There is nothing good about malls.

e. Other: _____

PART I

Predict

A. Quickly skim the two articles. Circle the answers.

Which article . . .

1. gives the writer's opinion?

    Reading 1   Reading 2   Readings 1 & 2

2. says good things about shopping malls?

    Reading 1   Reading 2   Readings 1 & 2

3. sounds like an advertisement?

    Reading 1   Reading 2   Readings 1 & 2

4. talks about a scientific study?

    Reading 1   Reading 2   Readings 1 & 2

B. Write a question that you think each article will answer.

Reading 1: _____

Reading 2: _____

Read It

Read the articles. Look for the answers to your questions.

 (**READING 1**)   Addicted to the Mall

What do you do for recreation? Do you swim, dance, play cards, garden, or read? Many people today prefer to spend their free time shopping. These people are called *recreational shoppers.* Recreational shoppers

do not always buy something. They really enjoy the shopping experience.

Of course, many people like going to indoor malls. However, for recreational shoppers, the mall is more than stores. For them, the mall represents happiness and fulfillment. For these people, a visit to the mall is an adventure. In fact, for many recreational shoppers the art of looking for and buying something is more fun than owning it.

Recently, a group of psychologists studied recreational shopping. First, they used tests to identify recreational shoppers. Then they compared recreational shoppers with ordinary shoppers. The psychologists discovered that the two groups were different. Recreational shoppers were usually younger, less self-confident, and more often female. In addition, they were more interested in material things and had less self-control.

The recreational shoppers also went shopping when they felt worried, angry, or depressed. Ordinary shoppers didn't. Most of the recreational shoppers said buying something helped them feel better—it made them happy. Their negative feelings went away. Many recreational shoppers also did something unusual while they were shopping. They pretended that they were different people with different lives.

Of course, shopping is an important part of our contemporary consumer society. We spend a lot of time in malls. In a recent study, people spent most of their time at home, at work, and in school. Shopping malls ranked fourth. However, in the future, will we think of recreational shopping as an addiction like smoking or drinking?

Palm Desert Mall: Where Dreams Come True!

Palm Desert Mall is the biggest and the best place to shop in Southern California! It offers visitors true *shoppertainment.* At Palm Desert, we combine stores, entertainment, restaurants, and fun. Shoppers say they're addicted to Palm Desert.

Palm Desert Mall has over 250 department stores, specialty shops, restaurants, entertainment venues, and carts and kiosks—all under one roof. And that roof is BIG. It is as large as 43 football fields!

For entertainment, moviegoers can choose from 53 movies! Palm Desert Mall also has many different special events every week. There are concerts, fashion shows, parties, and parades.

There are restaurants for everyone's taste and pocketbook. Do you want a formal restaurant for a special evening? Try Karen's Kitchen for gourmet salads or Western Grill for delicious baby-back ribs. Are you looking for delicious fish? The freshest seafood is at Captain Ahab's. And Palm Desert, of course, has a Mocha Java for delicious coffee. For informal dining, the Food Court has a world of choices. You can have Mexican tacos at La Salsa, Chinese egg rolls at Panda Express, or Thai curry at The Dusitani. And let's not forget American food. Since its 1996 opening, Palm Desert's Burger Boy has served more than 161,000 hamburgers.

Palm Desert Mall welcomes millions of visitors each year. Come and see how we can make your dreams come true!

Reading Comprehension

Check Your Predictions

1. Look back at questions 1–4 in the Predict section. How correct were your predictions?

Predictions	Not very correct	Correct
1		
2		
3		
4		

2. If you found the answers to your questions, what were they?

Reading 1: _____

Reading 2: _____

Reading Comprehension
Check the Facts

READING 1

A. Read the statements and write *true* (T) or *false* (F). Go back to Reading 1 and look for the answers you are unsure of.

_____ 1. All people who shop are recreational shoppers.

_____ 2. Recreational shoppers go shopping for fun.

_____ 3. Recreational shoppers love to own things.

_____ 4. Most shoppers dislike shopping.

_____ 5. Psychologists compared ordinary shoppers and recreational shoppers.

_____ 6. Recreational shoppers go shopping when they are sad.

_____ 7. Most recreational shoppers are men.

_____ 8. People spend more time in shopping malls than they do at work.

B. Answer the questions.

1. Compare the two groups and check the correct box.

	more materialistic	older	more self-confident	have less self-control
recreational shoppers				
ordinary shoppers				

2. Circle all that apply. While they are shopping, recreational shoppers . . .

   a. feel upset.

   b. pretend they are different people.

   c. are excited.

   d. steal things.

READING 2

A. Read the statements and write *true* **(T) or** *false* **(F). Go back to Reading 2 and look for the answers you are unsure of.**

_____1. Palm Desert Mall is in California.

_____2. This mall has more than 250 different places to spend money.

_____3. The mall has 43 different buildings.

_____4. It has 12 different movie theaters.

_____5. Some restaurants at the mall are expensive.

_____6. Karen's Kitchen is a cooking store.

B. Answer the questions.

1. Where can you find the inexpensive restaurants at the mall?

2. What can you do at Palm Desert Mall?

Analyze

1. Would recreational shoppers like Palm Desert Mall?
    Why or why not?

2. How does the writer of Reading 1 feel about recreational shopping?
    How do you know?

Vocabulary Work

Guess Meaning from Context

1. Look at these words from Reading 1. First, guess their part of speech. Then try to guess the meaning of each word.

	Part of speech	Meaning
a. identify	_____	_____
b. ordinary	_____	_____
c. material	_____	_____
d. negative	_____	_____
e. pretended	_____	_____
f. contemporary	_____	_____

2. An important skill in reading is to know when the exact meaning of a word is <u>not</u> important. Look at the <u>underlined</u> words in this selection from Reading 2. There may not be enough information to guess the complete meaning of each one. Which words can you guess? What clues did you use? Can you guess an approximate meaning for the other words? Put the numbered words in one of these three categories.

- a kind of activity
- a kind of place
- a kind of food

Palm Desert Mall has over 250 department stores, specialty shops, restaurants, entertainment <u>venues</u>, and <u>carts and kiosks</u>—all under one
1   2
<u>roof</u>. It is as large as 43 football fields! For entertainment, moviegoers can
3
choose from 53 movies! Palm Desert Mall also has many special events every week. There are concerts, <u>fashion shows</u>, parties, and parades. Try
4
Karen's Kitchen for gourmet salads, or Western Grill for delicious
<u>baby-back ribs</u>.
5

3. Sometimes grammar can help you guess the approximate meaning of unknown words.
- happiness and fulfillment

Is <u>fulfillment</u> probably something positive or negative?
- worried, angry, or depressed

Is <u>depressed</u> probably something good or bad?

Guess Meaning from Related Words

1. The following words are in the readings. Find other words that are related to them.

Reading 1

addicted _____

recreation _____

happy _____

Reading 2

special   _____

informal   _____

2. Work in pairs. Draw a chart like this one in your notebook. Put the words from Exercise 1 in the correct columns. Compare your work with another pair when you are done.

Noun (person)	Noun (thing)	Verb	Adjective	Adverb

3. Find common words or parts of common words inside these compound words. Many times this will help you guess the meaning of unknown words. In one of the words below, knowing the individual words *doesn't* help. Which word is it?

Reading 2

shoppertainment   _____

moviegoers   _____

seafood   _____

pocketbook   _____

Reading Skills

Identifying the Author's Purpose

What is the author's purpose in each article? Why do you think so?

To teach readers how to do something.

To inform readers about something.

To describe something to readers.

To persuade readers to do something.

Reading 1   Author's purpose: _____

Reading 2   Author's purpose: _____

Discussion

1. Do you think shopping can be an addiction? Why or why not?
2. Would you like to go to Palm Desert Mall? Why or why not?

PART II

Read the next article to find the answers to these questions.

1. According to the writer, are we all consumers?
2. What kinds of consuming do people do?
3. What kinds of experiences are more important—consuming experiences or nonconsuming experiences? Why?
4. How can we change our lives?

 READING

A Personal Reflection on Consumerism

By Kathy Fairclough
Used by permission.

How important is shopping to you? How many hours of your life do you spend earning money to buy things? How much time do you spend shopping for these things? And how much time do you spend organizing these things in your home? In the future, how much time will you use up spending money—in movie theaters, at amusement parks, at drive-thrus, at shopping malls, at convenience stores, at the gas <u>pump</u>, or at your desk paying bills? When you add it all up, you will probably see that you spend a lot of your life consuming *stuff*. Consuming products is not necessarily bad. However, since we spend so much time doing it, we should look at it carefully.

Imagine that you have a week off from school or work. You don't have to go to the office or go to class. However, in this week, you cannot spend any money—no shopping, no movies, no amusement park rides, no eating out. How would you spend your time? What things would bring you happiness? Perhaps you would take a walk on the beach with your best friend. Maybe you would climb a tree. You might just sit outside and enjoy the sunshine. Maybe you would play with your dog. Maybe you would draw a picture or write a story. Perhaps you would read a book, have a conversation with a stranger, or help a child read. You might sleep under the stars, daydream, or spend time with your family.

On our deathbeds, it is likely that nonconsuming experiences like these will be our most important memories. Why? Nonconsuming activities are active, not passive. They don't come in a package. You make the experience yourself. For example, each person who reads to a child will have a different experience. The experience changes with the reader, the child, and the book. However, if you watch a movie with a friend, you will each have a *packaged experience.* It requires no action and little interaction between the two of you. When you take a walk and have a conversation with a friend, however, you are actively *creating* an experience. The conversation that you have with your friend cannot be experienced or recreated by anyone else.

The consumerist environment we live in encourages us to have packaged experiences. We feel that we must consume because we believe that buying is doing. When we say to our friends, "Hey, let's do something," we usually mean, "let's spend money." However, we can start a personal revolution against consumerism. How? By consuming less. We can ask ourselves what experiences bring us the greatest satisfaction? Then we can organize our lives so that we have more of those kinds of experiences. The capitalist system can use us or we can use it. It's our choice.

Vocabulary Work

Guess Meaning from Related Words

Find all the words in Reading 3 related to these words.

1. consume   _____   _____   _____

2. action   _____   _____

3. create   _____

4. package   _____

Guess Meaning from Context

How can you use *world knowledge* to guess the approximate meaning of the <u>underlined</u> words?

In the future, how much time will you use up spending money—in movie

theaters, at <u>amusement parks</u>, at <u>drive-thrus</u>, at shopping malls, at
              1   2

<u>convenience stores</u>, at the gas <u>pump</u>, or at your desk paying bills?
 3   4

Reading Skills

Read for Main Ideas

Write the main ideas next to the correct paragraph.

- Explanation of why consuming activities aren't special
- Introduction—we consume most of the time
- Call to action
- Explanation of why nonconsuming activities are special

Paragraph 1 _____

_____

Paragraph 2 _____

_____

Paragraph 3 _____

_____

Paragraph 4 _____

_____

Idea Exchange

Think about Your Ideas

1. Do you enjoy shopping? If so, what kinds of things do you like to shop for?

   _____

2. How often do you . . .

	Never	Rarely	Some-times	Often
window shop?				
go shopping with friends?				
order things from catalogs?				
shop on the Internet?				
put off buying things because you hate to shop?				

3. What do you like about shopping? What do you dislike about shopping?

   Likes   Dislikes

   _____   _____

   _____   _____

Talk about Your Ideas

Discuss the answers to these questions.

1. How important is shopping in your life? Are you a recreational shopper?

2. Do you think that recreational shopping is bad? Why or why not?

3. What would you do with your free time if you couldn't go shopping for a month?

For CNN video activities about shopping and kids, turn to page 172.

CHAPTER 5

Las Vegas: Sin City

PREVIEW

Discuss the answers to these questions.

1. What do you think of when you hear the name *Las Vegas*?
2. Would you like to visit Las Vegas? Why or why not?

PART I

Predict

A. Quickly skim the two articles. Circle the answers.

Which article . . .

1. gives events in time order?

   Reading 1   Reading 2   Readings 1 & 2

2. is probably a description?

   Reading 1   Reading 2   Readings 1 & 2

3. wants you to buy something?

   Reading 1   Reading 2   Readings 1 & 2

4. gives a positive view of Las Vegas?

   Reading 1   Reading 2   Readings 1 & 2

B. Write a question that you think each article will answer.

Reading 1: _____

Reading 2: _____

Read It

Read the articles. Look for the answers to your questions.

 READING 1   The Strip

This is a picture of the *strip*. It's the most famous street in Las Vegas. It was the home of the first hotel and gambling casino in the city first named *El Rancho Vegas*. Other early hotels included The Last Frontier, Thunderbird, and Club Bingo. But the most famous one was the Flamingo. Mobster "Bugsy" Siegel built it in 1946.

This was not unusual at the time. The American mafia built many lavish hotels on the strip, including the Aladdin Casino, Circus Circus, The Sands, and The Tropicana. These hotels were popular. Their casinos offered free entertainment all night, so customers liked them. The gangsters liked them, too. They laundered their *dirty* money in the casinos and the businesses made profit.

Organized crime is not very important in Las Vegas anymore. Why? The capitalists bought out the mobsters. In the 1980s, businessmen saw that the casinos were profitable. The mafiosi sold their casinos and moved away. Some longtime Las Vegans are sorry. They say Las Vegas was better with the mob in charge. The food was cheaper and everyone had more fun.

Today, Las Vegas has customers coming for many different reasons. It is a popular vacation destination for people from around the world. There are nonstop flights from Tokyo, Japan; Seoul, South Korea; and Berlin, Germany. The yearly profit from gambling is over eight billion dollars.

Gambling is not the only profitable business in the city. In the year 1953, hotel rooms cost between three and eight dollars a night. Today, tourists pay up to $400 for a luxury room. The image of the Las Vegas strip is different, too. Of course, gambling, prostitution, and no-wait weddings are still legal here. However, ritzy hotels also offer fine dining, classy shops, and luxurious health spas. The gamblers still come, but tourists looking for a relaxing time come, too.

 READING 2

The Tiny White Wedding Chapel— Where Dreams Come True

Would you like an unusual wedding quickly? Do you want a memorable event that is also inexpensive? All this is possible! Come see us at the Tiny White Wedding Chapel. We will make your dreams come true. Your wedding can be large and lavish or small and sophisticated. If you want, you can have a simple, candlelighted ceremony. But, if you would prefer something unusual or spectacular, we have theater sets, smoke machines, special lighting, and costumes.

One of our most popular weddings is our Elvis Presley package. An Elvis impersonator performs the ceremony and sings some of Presley's hit songs. Or perhaps you would like to get married in another time and place. You can have an Egyptian wedding with King Tut performing the ceremony. You can go back to the time of King Arthur or have a wedding in outer space. Remember—the choice is yours. If you can imagine it, we can do it. The possibilities are endless. Explore them all at the Tiny White Wedding Chapel.

Each wedding package includes

- free limousine service

- free flowers

- free pictures

- free video of your wedding

- free marriage license information

- free traditional wedding music

Reading Comprehension

Check Your Predictions

1. Look back at questions 1–4 in the Predict section. How correct were your predictions?

Prediction	Incorrect	Correct
1		
2		
3		
4		

2. If you found the answers to your questions, what were they?

Reading 1: _____

Reading 2: _____

Check the Facts

READING 1

A. Read the statements and write *true* (T) or *false* (F). Go back to Reading 1 and look for the answers you are unsure of.

_____ 1. The strip is a street with a lot of hotels.

_____ 2. "Bugsy" Siegel built the first hotel and gambling casino on the strip.

_____ 3. Gangsters built many hotels in Las Vegas.

_____ 4. The mafia is very important in Las Vegas today.

_____ 5. Businessmen own many of the hotels.

_____ 6. Hotels in Las Vegas are expensive.

_____ 7. You can get married in Las Vegas very quickly.

_____ 8. Not many foreign tourists visit Las Vegas.

B. Answer the questions.

1. Write two ways that Las Vegas was different in the 1940s and 1950s from the way it is today.

   _____

   _____

2. Write two ways that Las Vegas is the same as it was in 1950.

   _____

   _____

READING 2

A. Read the statements and write *true* (T) or *false* (F). Go back to Reading 2 and look for the answers you are unsure of.

_____ 1. You can get married at the Tiny White Wedding Chapel.

_____ 2. You can have an inexpensive wedding at the Tiny White Wedding Chapel.

_____ 3. The chapel only has room for small weddings.

_____ 4. Some customers like unusual weddings.

_____ 5. King Arthur was an Egyptian.

_____ 6. You don't have to pay for flowers at the Tiny White Wedding Chapel.

B. Answer these questions.

1. Find four different kinds of weddings in the reading.

   _____

   _____

   _____

   _____

2. What special things does the Tiny White Wedding Chapel offer?

   _____

   _____

Analyze

Answer the questions. Give reasons for your answers.

1. How are Readings 1 and 2 related?
2. Why are weddings so popular in Las Vegas?
3. Is Elvis Presley very popular in Las Vegas?

Vocabulary Work

Guess Meaning from Context

1. A writer sometimes uses different names for the same noun.

gangster	mafia	Mafiosi
mob	mobster	organized crime

   Which two words and one phrase means "a group of criminals"?

   _____   _____   _____

   Which three words rename the criminals?

   _____   _____   _____

2. The writer in Reading 1 uses these words to describe the hotels in Las Vegas. What do they mean?

Words	Meaning
lavish	_____
ritzy	_____
luxurious	_____
classy	_____

3. Can you guess the meaning of this phrase?

> laundered their *dirty* money

4. Match these words to their meanings. What clues did you use?

Reading 1

1. casino
2. capitalists
3. in charge
4. destination
5. profit
6. image
7. prostitution
8. bought out

a. picture in your mind
b. place to go
c. a place to gamble
d. took over
e. businessmen
f. the sale of sex
g. the head of something
h. revenue

Reading 2

1. come true
2. sophisticated
3. spectacular
4. theater set

a. scenery for a play
b. happen
c. cultivated, educated
d. amazing to look at

Guess Meaning from Related Words

1. The following words are in the readings. Find other words that are related to them.

Reading 1

yearly _____

luxury _____

profit _____

Reading 2

remember_____

possible _____

2. Work in pairs. Draw a chart like this one in your notebook. Put the words from Exercise 1 in the correct columns. Compare your work with another pair when you are done.

Noun (person)	Noun (thing)	Verb	Adjective	Adverb

3. Circle the common words or parts of words inside these compound words and hyphenated words. Then guess the meanings of the original words.

Word	Meaning
longtime	_____
no-wait	_____
nonstop	_____
candlelighted	_____

Reading Skills

Understanding Organization

Reading 1 has two major parts.

1. What is the main idea of each one?

   _____

2. What divides the two parts? Look for grammatical clues.

   _____

3. What idea does each paragraph discuss?

   _____

   _____

Discussion

1. What is the best aspect of Las Vegas?
2. Are there any aspects of Las Vegas that you do not like?

PART II

Read the next article to complete the chart. Write an "X" if there is no information.

	Married? Children?	Advantages of the job	Disadvantages of the job	Future plans
Dina				
Sherona				
Yolanda				

 READING

The Lives of Vegas Strippers
by Karen DiMarco

LAS VEGAS—Being a stripper in Las Vegas has some advantages. The jobs are legal and well paid. However, stripping can be difficult. Last week, I had a chance to interview Dina, Yolanda, and Sherona—experienced strippers at a club in Las Vegas.

Karen: How did you start working in a strip club, Dina?

Dina: I was married and working as a waitress. Then my husband took off. I had two kids at home and I needed to make more money. Now I make double what I did in the restaurant.

Karen: What do your children think?

Dina: Sammy's just seven, so he doesn't think anything. Sandra is eleven. She still thinks that I'm a waitress. I'm going to quit before I have to tell her.

Karen: What do you think of this job, Sherona?

Sherona: Well, it wasn't my plan. I came to Las Vegas to work as a croupier in a casino, but I prefer this. I enjoy dancing. I don't have to worry about what folks think because my family is far away. I make good money and have a good time. Of course, I won't do this forever. I get tired of the men sometimes. I'm studying to be a real estate agent. After I start selling houses, I'll quit stripping, get married, and have kids.

Karen: Do some people do that? Do they get good jobs after working as strippers?

Yolanda: Sometimes. We had a girl here last year who loved animals. She worked for a veterinarian during the day and danced at night. Then she got promoted. They made her the manager of the vet clinic, so she left the club.

Karen: How common is that?

Dina: Not very common. Some go the other way. They get mixed up with drugs and prostitution. That's really sad.

Karen: Yolanda, you're married, aren't you?

Yolanda: Yeah. My husband is a security guard at one of the big casinos.

Karen: What does he think about your job?

Yolanda: He doesn't mind. He knows that it's just a job. He tells people that his wife is an exotic dancer. He says that all his buddies at work are green. Of course, he won't tell them where I dance. He doesn't want his friends in here. We're saving money for a house. When we have enough, I'll quit and we'll have kids.

Karen: Does he come watch you dance?

Yolanda: Yeah. About once a week. He's a really big guy. When the men know he's my husband, they leave me alone.

Karen: What about the customers? Are they a problem, Sherona? You don't have a husband to scare them off.

Sherona: Some of them think that strippers are prostitutes, so they don't understand when we say, "Hands off." But I'm rarely afraid. I wear seven-inch heels, so I'm taller than most of them. And Mr. K—he's the bouncer. He makes sure that they stay in line. If they don't, he just shows them the door.

Vocabulary Work

Guess Meaning from Context

Find the names of nine different jobs in the reading. Can you guess what each one does? Does it matter if you don't understand the meaning of each one?

_____   _____   _____

_____   _____   _____

_____   _____   _____

Reading Skills

Understanding Informal Language

People speak differently than they write. When you read an interview, you are reading spoken language. Some of the vocabulary and some of the grammar will be informal.

Write the meanings in the correct blank.

children	don't touch	obey the rules	makes them leave
involved with	jealous	left	a good salary
man	friends	people	two times as much

1. Then my husband <u>took off</u>.   _____
2. Now I make <u>double</u>.   _____
3. I don't have to worry about what <u>folks</u> think.   _____
4. I make <u>good money</u>.   _____
5. They get <u>mixed up with</u> drugs and prostitution.   _____
6. He says that all his <u>buddies</u> at work are <u>green</u>.   _____
   _____
7. When we have enough, I'll quit and we'll have <u>kids</u>.   _____
8. He's a really big <u>guy</u>.   _____
9. They don't understand when we say, "<u>Hands off</u>."   _____
10. He makes sure that they <u>stay in line</u>.   _____
11. He just <u>shows them the door</u>.   _____

Idea Exchange

Think about Your Ideas

What do you think of when you hear "Las Vegas"? Circle five words you think of. Add any other words that come to mind.

gambling	religious	beautiful	art	luxury	girls
weddings	modern	conservative	families	cheap	sin
money	tourists	magic	modern	lawless	desert

Talk about Your Ideas

1. Would you like to vacation in Las Vegas? Why or why not?
2. Would you like to live in Las Vegas? Why or why not?

For CNN video activities about gambling, turn to page 173.

CHAPTER 6

Shoplifting: Why is the price tag still on your hat?

PREVIEW

Complete these sentences. Then compare your guesses with a partner.

1. There are about _____ million shoplifters in the United States.

   10   23   40   65

2. About _____ percent of shoplifters are children; _____ percent are adults.

   15   25   75   85

3. Shoplifters say store owners catch them once in every _____ times they steal.

   10   23   48   62

4. About _____ percent of shoplifters don't plan to steal.

   70   50   30

5. _____ percent of shoplifters say they steal every day.

   Thirteen   Twenty-nine   Forty   Fifty-three

(Answers to Preview questions appear on the next page.)

PART I

Predict

A. Quickly skim these two articles. Circle the answers.

Which article . . .

1. explains why people shoplift?

   Reading 1   Reading 2   Readings 1 & 2

2. gives advice?

   Reading 1   Reading 2   Readings 1 & 2

3. divides shoplifters into groups?

   Reading 1   Reading 2   Readings 1 & 2

4. discusses teenaged shoplifters?

   Reading 1   Reading 2   Readings 1 & 2

B. Write a question that you think each article will answer.

Reading 1: _____

Reading 2: _____

Preview answers: **1.** 23 **2.** 25; 75 **3.** 48 **4.** 70 **5.** Thirteen

---

Read It

Read the articles. Look for the answers to your questions.

 (READING 1)   Different Types of Shoplifters

Terrence Shulman used to shoplift. Now he helps shoplifters stop stealing. He divides shoplifters into six types.

Compulsive Shoplifters: 85%

For these people, shoplifting is a compulsion. They can't stop themselves. These shoplifters often have other compulsive behaviors such as overeating, shopping, drug use, or gambling. They often don't take care of themselves. Usually they steal items that are inexpensive. Then they give

these things to others as gifts. If they are caught, they are very emotional—
they might cry and feel shame.

Professionals—People Who Steal For Profit: 2%

Professional shoplifters steal expensive items. They often take many
items at the same time. Many of them use special tools. If the police catch
them, they will try to run away. If they can't escape, they show no emotion.
They are cool, calm, and collected. They never feel guilty.

The Poor–People Who Steal Because They Have No Money: 5%

These shoplifters usually steal necessities like food, baby diapers,
toiletries, or children's clothing. If they are caught, they will say that they
are sorry. However, they will also explain that they have no money. They
may be angry at society because they are poor. They believe shoplifting is
necessary to support themselves and their families.

Thrill Seekers—People Who Steal for Excitement: 5%

These shoplifters will often steal in groups. Many teenagers belong to
this type. They steal because it's exciting. Teenagers steal clothes, CDs,
makeup, and computer games. They often feel afraid if the police catch them.

Drug Addicts: 2%

Like professionals, they take expensive items. Then they sell these things
to get money to buy drugs. They are usually less careful than the
professionals. If they are caught, they will try to run away.

Kleptomaniacs—Those Who Steal for No Reason: 1%

Kleptomaniacs are impulsive. They don't think before they act. They are
also often careless. They will often take items they don't need and can't use.
For example, they might steal shoes that don't fit. If they are caught, they
will usually admit they are kleptomaniacs. They do not feel guilty and they
are not ashamed. They will often give excuses like, "I don't know why I
took it because I don't even need it."

 READING 2   Young Shoplifters

Is shoplifting a serious problem?

Store owners lose almost $10 billion a year to shoplifters. As a result,
they must charge higher prices. So, you and your family are paying for the
things shoplifters take. There is no typical shoplifter—people of every sex,
age, race, and socioeconomic background steal from stores. But a large
percentage of shoplifters are teenagers. About 25 percent of all the people
who get caught shoplifting are between the ages of 13 and 17.

Why do teens shoplift?

Experts at Shoplifters Anonymous say that teens shoplift because they

a. think the stores don't need the money;
b. think they won't get caught;
c. can't stop themselves when they want something;
d. feel pressure from shoplifting friends;
e. are angry, frustrated, or sad.

Unfortunately, shoplifting can easily become an addiction. Some shoplifters say that they feel *high* when they steal. Because they feel good, they keep shoplifting. It's a habit that's hard to stop.

What should I do if my friend shoplifts?

Talk to your friend, but don't judge. Explain that you are worried. Help him or her find help. There are many programs for shoplifting such as telephone hot lines, programs in hospitals, and community health services. If your friend won't stop shoplifting, don't shop with him or her. If the police catch your friend, they will think that you are a shoplifter, too. Although this "guilt by association" may not be fair, it happens.

Reading Comprehension

Check Your Predictions

1. Look back at questions 1–4 in the Predict section. How correct were your predictions?

Prediction	Correct	Not correct
1		
2		
3		
4		

2. If you found the answers to your questions, what were they?

Reading 1: _____

Reading 2: _____

Check the Facts

READING 1

A. Read the statements and write *true* (T) or *false* (F). Go back
   to Reading 1 and look for the answers you are unsure of.

_____ 1. All shoplifters are the same.

_____ 2. Shoplifters are usually poor.

_____ 3. Professional shoplifters don't feel guilty.

_____ 4. Poor people steal expensive items.

_____ 5. Kleptomaniacs are often careless.

_____ 6. Professionals may use tools.

B. Complete the table. Write "?" if you do not know the information.

Type of shoplifter	Percentage of shoplifters that are this type	Reasons they steal	Items they steal	What they do if they are caught	Feelings they have if they are caught
Compulsive shoplifters					
Professionals					
The poor					
Thrill seekers					
Drug addicts					
Kleptomaniacs					

READING 2

A. Read the statements and write *true* (T) or *false* (F). Go back
   to Reading 2 and look for the answers you are unsure of.

_____ 1. Women shoplift more often than men.

_____ 2. Most shoplifters are teenagers.

_____ 3. The cost of shoplifting is about $10 billion a year.

_____ 4. Teenagers sell the things they steal.

_____ 5. Shoplifting makes some people feel good.

_____ 6. Some shoplifters are addicted to stealing.

Shoplifting: Why is the price tag still on your hat?

B. Circle all the correct answers.

1. Many teenagers shoplift because
   a. they are sad or angry.
   b. they want things.
   c. their friends shoplift.
   d. they want to get caught.
2. If your friend shoplifts,
   a. call the police.
   b. tell his or her parents.
   c. help him or her find a program that helps shoplifters.
   d. don't go shopping with him or her.
   e. give him or her money to buy things.

Analyze

Answer these questions. Give reasons for your answers.

1. Do kleptomaniacs care if they are caught?
2. Which group is similar to drug addicts?
3. Compare the statistics about teenagers in the two readings. Are they the same?

Vocabulary Work

Guess Meaning from Context

1. Sometimes example sentences can help you guess the meaning of a word. What sentences from Reading 1 may help you understand these words and phrases?

   compulsive behaviors   _____

   emotional   _____

   necessities   _____

2. It is often not necessary to understand each item in a list—the list gives you a general idea of the meaning. What is an approximate meaning for these words found in lists in Reading 1?

   collected   _____

   makeup   _____

   hot line   _____

3. Sometimes you can guess the meaning of unknown words or phrases by looking backward or forward in the text for the definition. What is the meaning of these two items?
   - high (*Hint:* Look forward in the text.)
   - this guilt by association (Hint: Look backward in the text.)

Guess Meaning from Related Words

1. The following words are in the readings. Find other words that are related to them in the readings.
   a. shoplift   _____   _____
   b. compulsive   _____
   c. inexpensive _____
   d. emotion   _____
   e. guilt   _____
   f. shame   _____
   g. exciting   _____
   h. necessary   _____

2. Work in pairs. Draw a chart like this one in your notebook. Put the words from Exercise 1 in the correct columns. Compare your work with another pair when you are done.

Noun (person)	Noun (thing)	Verb	Adjective	Adverb

Reading Skills

Using Headings and Subtitles

Writers often use headings and subtitles to help the reader. They are like signs on a road. They tell you what's coming.

1. Look at Reading 1. What is each subtitle?
   a. How do the subtitles help you understand the organization of the reading?
   b. How do they help you understand what is coming?
2. Look at Reading 2. What is each subtitle?
   a. How do the subtitles help you understand the organization of the reading?
   b. How do they help you understand what's coming?

Discussion

1. Do you think shoplifting is a big problem? Why or why not?
2. What kinds of things do store owners do to stop shoplifters?
3. Have you ever seen anyone shoplift? If so, what did you do?

PART II

This reading is more difficult than the articles in Part I. Read it for the main ideas. Do not worry if you cannot understand everything.

Read to find the answers to these questions.

1. Why are holidays stressful for kleptomaniacs?
2. Why are holidays difficult for store owners?
3. How does shoplifting hurt everyone?
4. What is CASA?
5. Why do people go to CASA?

 READING

Holiday Stress Is Worse for Kleptomaniacs

Springfield, Ohio; November 28—Although the holidays are stressful for many people, kleptomaniacs have an even greater problem than most of us. They are afraid to go shopping because they have a compulsion to steal. Large crowds make holiday shopping time difficult for store owners, too. As stores become more crowded, store detectives have a harder time watching the customers. The president of the state's store owners' association, Larry Mason, says that there is also an increased problem with shoplifting. "During the holiday season, we have more shoppers, more sales, and more shoplifting—the problem is worse because of the number of sales."

People shoplift for a variety of reasons. Some steal for profit and sell the merchandise afterwards. Others simply pick up an item because they don't have enough money—they can't afford to buy it. Others are addicted to shoplifting. Mason says that there is no average shoplifter. "There are shoplifting grandmothers, doctors, teachers, and even movie stars. Last year, actress Winona Ryder was caught shoplifting." In the same way, shoplifters might steal just about any kind of merchandise. Clothing, DVDs, and jewelry are at risk, but large items like skis and stereo equipment are also in danger. Store-owner groups say that more than $15 billion worth of merchandise walks out of store doors every year. And that's pricey news for customers since decreases in store profits mean increases in prices. According to one store-owner group, between three and five percent of the price of an item pays for security and stolen merchandise.

Five years ago, Terry Schulman formed CASA (Cleptomaniacs and Shoplifters Anonymous). He says his own addiction became so bad that he stole something every day. "The addictive-compulsive shoplifter, like myself and most of the people who come to the group, shoplift as a way to cope with life," Schulman says. CASA is a support group. Some people come because they have to—a judge has told them that they must. However, most people come because they want to get better. Many people at a recent CASA meeting were worried about the holidays. They said that the stress of the holidays and the need to shop increased the chance that they might steal.

As they left, Schulman smiled and said to them, "Keep coming back—that's the key phrase. Just keep coming back."

Vocabulary Work

Guess Meaning from Context

1. Find related words in the reading.

   stress   _____

   crowds   _____

   increase   _____

   pricey   _____

   stolen   _____

2. Can you guess the meaning of these words? What clues did you use?

detectives _____

merchandise _____

afford _____

at risk _____

judge _____

3. How is the meaning of the <u>underlined</u> phrase different from its normal meaning?

> Fifteen billion dollars worth of merchandise <u>walks out of</u> store doors every year.

Reading Skills

Using Grammar to Increase Understanding

Sometimes one section of a reading contains many examples of the same grammatical structure. This can help you if you know what that structure is used for. Look for a word that repeats and the words that follow.

Read the paragraph below. <u>Underline</u> all the comparisons.
Read the paragraph out loud if you can't find the comparisons.

Although the holidays are stressful for many people, kleptomaniacs have an even greater problem than average. Imagine being afraid to go shopping because you have a compulsion to steal. Large crowds in malls and stores make holiday shopping time more difficult for store owners, too. As stores become more crowded, store detectives have a harder time watching the customers. Larry Mason of the Ohio Store Owners' Union says that there is an increased problem with shoplifting. "During the holiday season, we have more shoppers and more shoplifting—the problem is worse because there are a lot more sales," he says.

Idea Exchange

Think about Your Ideas

1. Do you know anyone who shoplifts? Why do you think they do it?
2. What might make them stop?
3. Which of these solutions might reduce the problem of shoplifting?

	Probably not effective	Possibly effective	Probably effective
More security guards			
More cameras			
More laws			
Education			
Therapy			
Government help for the poor			

Talk about Your Ideas

1. Is shoplifting a problem in your culture? Why or why not?
2. If people shoplift, why do they do it?
3. How can each of these groups help stop shoplifting?
   a. police officers
   b. teachers
   c. store owners
   d. parents
   e. the government

For CNN video activities about a celebrity shoplifting scandal, turn to page 174.

CHAPTER 7

GLUTTONY:
YOU ARE WHAT YOU EAT!

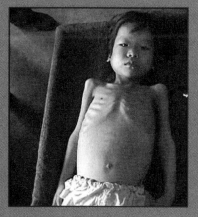

PREVIEW

Discuss the answers to these questions.

1. Which of these people are . . .
   a. probably hungry?
   b. unhealthy because they don't get enough food?
   c. unhealthy because they don't eat the right food?
   d. poor?
2. Which of these countries have problems with malnutrition?
   a. Great Britain
   b. Ethiopia
   c. the United States
   d. China
   e. India

(Answer is on page 74.)

PART I

Predict

A. Quickly skim these two articles. Circle the answers.

Which article . . .

1. gives statistics for overweight people?

   Reading 1   Reading 2   Readings 1 & 2

2. gives statistics for world hunger?

   Reading 1   Reading 2   Readings 1 & 2

3. explains why people are overweight?

   Reading 1   Reading 2   Readings 1 & 2

4. compares obesity and hunger?

   Reading 1   Reading 2   Readings 1 & 2

B. Write a question that you think each article will answer.

Reading 1: _____

Reading 2: _____

> The answer to question 2 on page 73 is that <u>all</u> of these countries
> have a problem with malnutrition.

Read It

Read the articles. Look for the answers to your questions.

 (**READING 1**)   The Hows and Whys of Gluttony

The dictionary says that a *glutton* is a person who eats too much. If so,
the United States is a nation of gluttons. Almost 65 percent of the
population is now overweight. About 31 percent, or 59 million people, are
obese—that is, they weigh more than 20 percent than they should. Experts
say that within five years, four out of ten Americans will be in this group. In
1989, 47 percent of Americans were overweight and 15 percent were obese.

We now know that gluttony is not just self-indulgent. Being overweight can cause serious health problems such as heart disease, high blood pressure, and diabetes. So, why are so many of us eating ourselves to death?

Experts in obesity research say there are a number of reasons. First, food is cheaper than it was in the past. They say that it is natural to eat when we can. Second, we lead very sedentary lives—we rarely move. Most of us have desk jobs. We don't walk to shops, schools, or banks—we drive cars. Furthermore, at home we have a lot of machines to *help* us. We don't push lawn mowers—we ride on them. We don't rake leaves—we blow them away with leaf blowers. We don't wash dishes anymore—the dishwasher does. In addition, robot vacuum cleaners clean our floors. And, of course, the television remote control means that we can sit in a chair for hours. We usually call these machines *labor-saving* devices. Maybe if we called them *fat-development* devices, people would stop using them.

 (**READING 2**)   Underfed and Overfed

The Worldwatch Institute says that the number of overweight people in the world equals the number of underweight people for the first time in history. Today there are about 1.1 billion people who are hungry. There are also about 1.1 billion people who are overweight.

Hunger is decreasing around the world. There are fewer starving people every year. In 1970, 35 percent of people in developing countries were suffering from starvation. By 1996, the figure was 18 percent. The United Nations says that it will be only 6 percent by 2030.

Unfortunately, the number of overweight people is increasing faster than the starvation rate is decreasing. In the United States, 55 percent of adults are overweight; 23 percent of American adults are considered obese. However, the United States is not alone. Surprisingly, excessive body weight and obesity are increasing rapidly in developing countries, too. The report states that in the past, people in these countries were unhealthy because they did not have enough to eat. Now they are unhealthy because they overeat.

Everyone understands that hunger is a problem. People who do not have enough to eat are malnourished. Their bodies do not get the nutrients they need. However, most people do not understand that many overweight people also suffer from malnutrition. According to the report, both the hungry and the overweight have health problems. They are sicker and die younger than other people.

Reading Comprehension

Check Your Predictions

1. Look back at questions 1–4 in the Predict section. How correct were your predictions?

Prediction	Correct	Not correct
1		
2		
3		
4		

2. If you found the answers to your questions, what were they?

Reading 1: _____

Reading 2: _____

Check the Facts

READING 1

A. Read the statements and write *true* (T) or *false* (F). Go back to Reading 1 and look for the answers you are unsure of.

_____ 1. Obese people are only a little overweight.

_____ 2. A glutton eats too much.

_____ 3. Being overweight causes hearing problems.

_____ 4. Food is less expensive than it was before.

_____ 5. Sedentary people are very active.

_____ 6. We eat more because there is more food.

B. Answer the questions.

1. What are the two main reasons why so many people are overweight?

   _____

   _____

2. Name some labor-saving devices.

   _____ _____ _____ _____

READING 2

A. Read the statements and write *true* (T) or *false* (F). Go back to Reading 2 and look for the answers you are unsure of.

_____ 1. Starving people are overweight.

_____ 2. Malnutrition is the same as malnourishment.

_____ 3. Starvation is decreasing.

_____ 4. About 1.1 billion people are starving.

_____ 5. Obesity is increasing faster than starvation is decreasing.

Analyze

Answer the questions. Give reasons for your answers.

1. What kinds of problems does obesity cause?
2. Compare the statistics in the two readings. Are they the same?
3. How does wealth cause obesity?
4. Is starvation a problem in rich countries? Why or why not?

Vocabulary Work

Guess Meaning from Context

1. Sometimes a writer gives readers a definition of an unknown word. What do these words mean?

   a. glutton _____

   b. obese _____

   c. sedentary _____

2. How will *world knowledge* help you to guess the meaning of these two words?

a. malnutrition _____

b. starvation _____

Guess Meaning from Related Words

1. The following words are in the readings. Find other words that are related to them.

Reading 1

weigh _____

obese _____

glutton _____

Reading 2

weight _____

overfed _____

nutrients _____

starving _____

hungry _____

2. Work in pairs. Draw a chart like this one in your notebook. Put the words from Exercise 1 in the correct columns. Compare your work with another pair when you are done.

Noun (person)	Noun (thing)	Verb	Adjective	Adverb

3. Find common words or parts of common words inside these compound words and phrases.

Reading 1

desk job

lawn mower

leaf blower

robot vacuum cleaner

television remote control

labor-saving

Reading 2

overweight

overeat

overfed

Reading Skills

Understanding Statistics

When a reading has a lot of numbers and other statistics, it is important to read carefully.

Almost 65 percent of the population is now overweight. About 31 percent, or 59 million people, are *obese*—that is, they weigh more than 20 percent than they should. Experts say that within five years, four out of ten Americans will be in this group. In 1989, 47 percent of Americans were overweight and 15 percent were obese.

Which numbers or statistics refer to:

overweight people _____ _____

obese people _____ _____ _____

_____ _____

Discussion

1. Which problem is more serious—starvation or obesity? Why?

2. In what ways could people try to increase their activity?

3. In your country, do people eat differently than they used to? Explain.

PART II

This reading is more difficult than the articles in Part I. Read it for the main ideas. Do not worry if you cannot understand everything.

Read to find the answers to these questions.

1. Where is obesity a problem?
2. What is a *toxic-food environment?*
3. Why does the writer think we eat unhealthy food?
4. How can we solve this health problem?

 READING   World Obesity—Whose Fault Is It?

The number of overweight people around the world is increasing. For example, in China the number rose from 9 percent to 15 percent between 1989 and 1992. The increases in Latin America and Europe were similar. However, the most worrying statistic is the increase of obesity in children. A new study by the World Health Organization (WHO) says that 3.3 percent of children are overweight. But some countries have much higher rates. In the United States, almost 33 percent of children under five are overweight. In some parts of Europe, the rate is almost 30 percent. Even developing countries have problems. In Egypt, Chile, Armenia, and Algeria, for example, the rate is well over 5 percent. In Uzbekistan it is almost 15 percent.

The problem is the change in our diets combined with the change in our lifestyles. We used to eat whole grains, vegetables, and fruit. Now we eat foods that contain a lot of fat and sugar. We consume many more calories than before, but we need many less. All those extra calories turn into fat.

Experts say that it is not surprising that people eat too much of the wrong foods. Everywhere we look there are advertisements for high-calorie, high-fat foods. These foods are low in nutrition but also low in cost. In other words, they may not be good for you, but they are really cheap. Some experts call this a *toxic-food environment.*

Most of us do not recognize this unhealthy environment. Therefore, we believe if you are fat, it's your responsibility. This is not completely true. We learn a lot about food from advertising. The most well-advertised foods are usually the least nutritious. Unfortunately, a great number of advertisements are made for children. In the United States, the average child watches 10,000 television advertisements each year. More than 90 percent of these advertise sugary cereals, candy, soda, and other junk foods.

Today, many food corporations are focusing on developing countries. In 1998, one soft-drink company told its stockholders that. "Africa is a land of opportunity for us." The number of fast-food restaurants around the world is also growing rapidly. The largest American fast-food company opens five new restaurants every day. Four of them are located outside the United States.

It is terrible to think that we may soon live in a world where everyone eats fast food and drinks soda. However, it is not unavoidable. Governments should educate their citizens about the dangers of eating the wrong food. This is particularly important for tomorrow's adults.

Vocabulary Work

Guess Meaning from Context

Can you guess the meanings of these words? What clues did you use?

Words: worrying   rates   consume

          turn into   toxic   junk foods   unavoidable

Clues:

1. It looks like a word I know.
2. I guessed it from the example the writer used.
3. I used my world knowledge.
4. There is a definition or a synonym in the reading.

Reading Skills

Main Ideas and Supporting Details

First, write the main idea of each paragraph.

Paragraph	Main idea	Type of supporting details
1		
2		
3		
4		
5		
6		

Next, identify the *type* of supporting details for each paragraph. Write the type of supporting detail above.

- statistics
- quotations
- reasons
- examples

Idea Exchange

Think about Your Ideas

How much responsibility does each group have for the increase in obesity?

	None	Very little	Some	A lot	Almost all
Individual adults					
Parents					
Children					
Government					
Doctors					
Schools					
Food manufacturers					
Advertisers					
Restaurants					

Talk about Your Ideas

1. What can each of the groups in the chart do to help people eat healthier food?

2. Not everyone agrees that obesity is a social problem. Do you agree or disagree with the opinion below?

> Look out for the food police. They are attacking a traditional American meal—a cheeseburger, an order of french fries, and a large soda. A Yale University professor wants to have a special tax on high-calorie foods such as french fries. The Center for Science in the Public Interest wants to put warning labels on soft drinks. Such acts are taking away our freedom of choice.

For CNN video activities about obesity worldwide, turn to page 175.

CHAPTER 8

Get-Rich-Quick $$$$ Scams: Have I got a deal for YOU!

CONTRACT

PREVIEW

Discuss the answers to these questions.

1. What are some ways that people try to make money without actually working?

2. Do you know anyone who *got rich quick*? How?

3. Do you know anyone who tried to get rich quick and lost money instead?

PART I

Predict

A. Quickly skim these two articles. Circle the answers.

Which article . . .

1. is critical of trying to *get rich quick?*

   Reading 1   Reading 2   Readings 1 & 2

2. tries to persuade the reader to do something?

   Reading 1   Reading 2   Readings 1 & 2

3. has information from people who agree and disagree?

   Reading 1   Reading 2   Readings 1 & 2

4. is probably from a newspaper?

   Reading 1   Reading 2   Readings 1 & 2

B. Write a question that you think each article will answer.

Reading 1: _____

Reading 2: _____

Read It

Read the articles. Look for the answers to your questions.

 READING 1

Get Rich or Get Conned?

PHILADELPHIA—Would you like to make thousands of dollars a month without working? Then Greg Cheney wants to talk to you.

You can see Greg on television every day. He is always selling something. Now he has a new product. He calls it the "greatest diet pill in the world." However, the "greatest diet pill" is really the "biggest scam" in the world.

"This is the easiest way in the world to make a fortune," says Cheney in his TV commercial. "If you get 20 people to try this product, we will send you a thousand dollars," the con artist promises. And some people believe him. "It sounded so good," says Kelly Eagan. "I signed up the same day."

The rip-off works like this. Cheney isn't really selling diet pills. He is selling Web sites that *advertise* diet pills. You buy a Web site. Then you wait for people to go to the Web site and buy the diet pills. However, the numbers don't work. The diet pills cost $39.95 a bottle. Twenty bottles cost about $800. How can Cheney pay the seller $1,000 to make $800? The answer is that he can't.

Cheney sells the Web sites for $35. But most people pay much more than that. After you sign up, he sells you a lot more things. Cheney says the extra things bring more customers to the Web sites. However, Kelly Eagan paid him $5,175 and only one person visited her site.

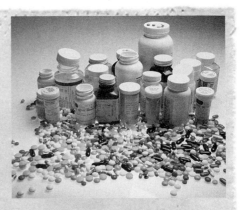

Cheney has a list of people who have made a lot of money. He says that he sends out checks every week—$3,500, $5,600, even $22,782. But even some people on the list have lost money. For example, Susan Kauffman is on the moneymaker list. She says she spent $5,000 and sold about 23 bottles of diet pills. Igor Spilsak is on the list, too. He paid $2,000 and sold six bottles of diet pills. However, in the commercial he says, "This is the easiest thing I've ever done and I'm making more than $100 an hour." Why did he lie? Cheney paid him $600 to be in the commercial.

Cheney insists that you can make money if you work hard and don't quit. However, it seems that only one person is getting rich quick and that's Greg Cheney.

Your Door to Wealth and Happiness!

Would you like to earn $3,000 to $7,000 a week without doing any work?

No meetings. No presentations. No questions to answer. No rejection. This is possible if you join our Power Profit Team.

On our team, you will learn to use the most powerful automated marketing system in the world. With this system, *anyone* can earn thousands of dollars a week. No matter if you are a student, a housewife, or an executive. **No experience is necessary.** Your profit is **<u>GUARANTEED</u>**.

A group of marketing professionals created this incredibly profitable system. These men and women have made a total **$20,000,000** on the Internet. They know how to market products. Let them teach *you*.

With our system, you can sell directly to **600 million Internet users.** That's a huge market. And you don't have to lift a finger. The program works 24 hours a day— seven days a week. It finds the customers and sells automatically. You don't have to sell. You don't have to answer questions. No one rejects you. And it never runs out of people.

Here's how the system works. You sign up seven people on your first day. Each person pays you $1,000. You keep $5,000 and send $2,000 to your sponsor. (Your sponsor is the person who told you about the program.) That may not sound good, but watch what happens.

The next day two of your people each sign up two more. The $2,000 from both these sales go to you. That's $4,000. Then those four each sign up two more people. That's **$8,000** more dollars in your pocket! **Your income will explode.** You may earn as much as $30,000 in your first three weeks. And you don't have to *do* anything. Just sit at home and watch the checks arrive!

When you sign on to our Power Profit Team, you will receive our wealth education package. This system of audiotapes, videotapes, and textbooks will teach you life lessons that only wealthy people know. **You will learn how to be happy and successful in every part of your life.**

Send us your e-mail address and we will send you more information and invite you to a special Internet question-and-answer program.

> *Don't delay. Do it today.*
> *Success and wealth are waiting for YOU!*

Reading Comprehension

Check Your Predictions

1. Look back at questions 1–4 in the Predict section. How correct were your predictions?

Prediction	Correct	Not correct
1		
2		
3		
4		

2. If you found the answers to your questions, what were they?

Reading 1: _____

Reading 2: _____

Check the Facts

READING 1

A. **Read the statements and write** *true* **(T) or** *false* **(F). Go back to Reading 1 and look for the answers you are unsure of.**

_____ 1. Greg Cheney makes diet pills.

_____ 2. Greg Cheney always tells the truth.

_____ 3. Many people have made a lot of money with Cheney's company.

_____ 4. Kelly Eagan lost money.

_____ 5. Most people pay only $35.

_____ 6. One bottle of diet pills cost $39.95.

_____ 7. Igor Spilsak lied in the TV commercial.

B. Complete the chart.

	Amount they paid	Amount they made	Amount they lost
Kelly Eagan			
Susan Kauffman			
Igor Spilsak			

How much money did Greg Cheney make from these people?

READING 2

Answer the questions according to the information in the reading.

1. What are the advantages of this program?
2. Who created the program?
3. If you sign up, what do you get?
4. Why should you sign up soon?

Analyze

Answer these questions. Give reasons for your answers.

1. How does the writer of Reading 1 feel about Greg Cheney? How do you know?
2. Who was Reading 2 written for?
3. Reading 2 does not tell you how much the program costs. Why not?
4. This reading is about a *pyramid scheme.* What might be wrong with this way of making money? Do you think it can work?

Vocabulary Work

Guess Meaning from Context

1. In Reading 1, the writer uses several words that mean "lying in order to cheat someone out of money." One word is *con.* Find two others.

   _____   _____

2. Use your *world knowledge* to guess the meaning of these words.

fortune   _____

sign up   _____

market   _____

professional _____

profit   _____

3. Sometimes the writer gives you the definition of a word. What does *sponsor* mean?

Guess Meaning from Related Words

1. The following words are in Reading 2. Find other words that are related to them.

a. rejection   _____

b. automated   _____

c. profitable   _____

d. market   _____

e. wealth   _____

f. successful   _____

2. Work in pairs. Draw a chart like this one in your notebook. Put the words from Exercise 1 in the correct columns. Compare your work with another pair when you are done.

Noun (person)	Noun (thing)	Verb	Adjective	Adverb

3. Find common words or parts of common words inside these words.

a. moneymaker   _____

b. con artist   _____

Reading Skills

Identifying the Author's Purpose

1. Which author informs readers? What information does the author want the readers to know?

2. Which author tries to persuade readers? What does the author want readers to do?

3. Look at Reading 1.

    a. How does the writer use quotes?

    b. Do you know the writer's opinion?

4. Look at Reading 2.

    a. How does the writer use punctuation and formatting?

    b. What positive words can you find?

    c. Do you know the writer's opinion? How?

Discussion

Answer the questions. Give reasons for your opinions.

1. "People who believe in get rich quick scams *should* lose their money." Do you agree with this statement? Why or why not?

2. Do you think that people today are more dishonest than they were in the past?

PART II

Read the next article to find the answers to these questions.

1. What is the purpose of groups like the Wise Women's Circle?

2. How much money does each woman on the bottom give?

3. How much money does the woman on the top get?

4. What happens after the woman at the top gets her money?

5. Why doesn't it work?

6. Why do women join these groups?

Doing Good for Others—Making Money for Yourself

DALTON RIVER—The Wise Women's Circle promises "true sisterhood" and a "strong backbone of energy." It's a scam, but it works. Suppose you are a woman and a good friend tells you about a new women's group. The purpose of the group is to help other women. You have to give $5,000 to a woman in need. Then in just a few days or maybe a week or two, you'll get $40,000. Doesn't it sound good? Wouldn't you do it?

Each group usually consists of 15 women. Although it is called a circle, it is actually a pyramid. There is one woman at the top. There are two under her. Then there are four beneath them and eight at the bottom of the pyramid. The woman at the top gets $40,000 when the bottom level of the pyramid is complete. She then leaves the pyramid, and the group divides itself into two more pyramids. All the members move up one level. Both groups must then find eight new members to complete the bottom level of the two new pyramids.

What's wrong with the plan? The math doesn't work. If each person must find eight people, then eight cycles requires the participation of more than 2 million people. A few more cycles and the number is greater than the entire population of the world. At least 90 percent of the participants will lose everything they put in.

It is not just poor or uneducated people who don't understand the math. In Dallas, Texas, a few years ago, professional-women *gifters* had meetings at their homes. The meetings often began with a pep talk about the benefits of the program. The speakers always explained how the group needed more women to keep the circle from breaking. The leaders also said that it was legal because the payments were gifts. At each meeting, one woman received a *birthday gift*—eight gift-wrapped packages. Each one contained $5,000.

Two women finally blew the whistle on the scam. They suddenly realized that the circle didn't help other women. It hurt them. They each gave $5,000. Then they invited friends and family to join. Two weeks later, it was time for their "birthday party." But before the meeting, they read a newspaper story about the scam. They then went to the police. "One lady was going to sell her jewelry and another lady was going to get the money from her credit card," one of the women told the *Dallas Express* in 2000.

Police investigators say that the "women helping women" idea is very powerful. They also usually support the safety of investing in women's businesses. Women think it is safe because they believe women don't hurt other women. Unfortunately, that is not always true.

Vocabulary Work

Guess Meaning from Related Words

1. Use related words to guess the meaning of these words.

    a. sisterhood _____

    b. backbone _____

    c. uneducated _____

    d. payment _____

    e. safety _____

2. Can you guess the meaning of these words? What clues did you use?

    a. in need _____

    b. pyramid _____

    c. cycles _____

    d. pep talk _____

    e. blew the whistle _____

Reading Skills

Understanding Organization

1. Match each purpose with the correct paragraph.

    a. conclusion

    b. introduction

    c. description of a specific group

    d. description of the plan in general

    e. problems with the plan in general

2. Write the most important or main idea for each paragraph.

Paragraph 1:

    Purpose: _____

    Most important idea: _____

Paragraph 2:

    Purpose: _____

    Most important idea: _____

Paragraph 3:

    Purpose: _____

    Most important idea: _____

Paragraphs 4 & 5:

    Purpose: _____

    Most important idea: _____

Paragraph 6:

    Purpose: _____

    Most important idea: _____

Idea Exchange

Think about Your Ideas

Here are some ways to make money. Check (✓) how you feel about each one.

	It's expensive to start.	It's easy to start.	It's risky.	It's safe.	It takes a long time to make money.
Lottery					
Pyramid scheme					
Internet deals					
Stock market					
Real estate					
Savings account					

Talk about Your Ideas

1. What are the good points (pros) and problems (cons) with the following:
   a. The lottery
   b. A pyramid scheme
   c. Internet deals
   d. The stock market
   e. Real estate
   f. A savings account

2. Do you agree or disagree with these statements? Why or why not?
   a. *There's nothing wrong with getting rich without working. People who buy stock are making money and they aren't working. Nobody wants to put them in jail.*
   b. *People who want to get rich quick deserve to lose their money. They're lazy and just don't want to work like the rest of us.*

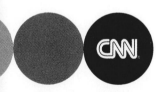

For CNN video activities, about "get-rich-quick" scams, turn to page 176.

CHAPTER 9

SPORTS DOPING: DOES IT MATTER IF YOU WIN OR LOSE?

a.

b.

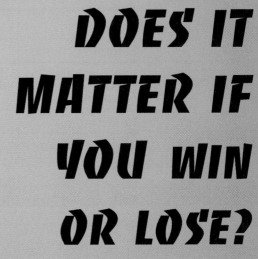

c.

d.

e.

PREVIEW

Look at the pictures of these athletes. Do you know any of them? What do they have in common?

(Answers are on the next page.)

PART I

Predict

A. Skim these two articles. Circle the answers.

Which article . . .

1. names athletes that got caught doping?

   Reading 1   Reading 2   Readings 1 & 2

2. names specific drugs that athletes use?

   Reading 1   Reading 2   Readings 1 & 2

3. says that doping in sports is a problem?

   Reading 1   Reading 2   Readings 1 & 2

4. talks about punishments for doping in sports?

   Reading 1   Reading 2   Readings 1 & 2

B. Write a question that you think each article will answer.

Reading 1: _____

Reading 2: _____

Answer to Preview question:

All of these athletes have been accused of sports doping including steroid use.

a. Track and field star athlete (running) Ben Johnson
b. Baseball star athlete Jason Giambi
c. Track and field star athlete (running) Marion Jones
d. Cyclist Christophe Moreau
e. Track and field star athlete (shotput) Kevin Toth

Read It

Read the articles. Look for the answers to your questions.

 (READING 1) The Problem of Sports Doping

Sports doping is becoming a bigger and bigger problem. Although there are many different drug tests, each year even more different kinds of drugs are available. In addition, more athletes are taking drugs to help their performance. And it's not just professional athletes. Even some teenagers take drugs to help their high school team win "the big game."

Athletes use drugs in a number of different ways. Some take drugs to make themselves stronger and faster. They also use drugs to mask pain, help them relax, or increase their confidence. But they all take drugs for the same reason—to win. For some, winning is more than just a gold medal. A star athlete can earn a lot of money. For others, winning just means *bragging rights*—they can talk big for a while. So, although athletes know that working hard is the way to win, they also know that drugs can give them a special advantage. Some of them also believe that *not* taking drugs is a disadvantage.

Below is a chart of the most common drugs that athletes use.

(Article continues on next page.)

Most of the drugs in the chart are banned in Olympic competitions; they are not allowed at all. However, some, such as cortisone, are only restricted in Olympic competition because they are sometimes necessary.

Using banned drugs can have many bad consequences. If an athlete is caught, he or she will not be allowed to compete. However, even if an athlete is not caught, these drugs are dangerous. For example, if athletes use drugs that mask pain, they may seriously injure themselves. Other banned drugs have even more serious consequences. Some drugs can cause heart attacks, strokes, and even cancer. Furthermore, injections that are not given by a doctor are always risky. Unclean conditions can lead to serious diseases such as HIV-AIDS and hepatitis. Unfortunately, more and more competitors are willing to take all of these risks in order to win.

 READING 2   Olympian Drug Problems

Many Olympians failed drug tests at the 2004 games in Athens. The following list shows that sports doping is definitely a global problem. The list is long; however, remember that more than 10,000 Olympic athletes competed in the 2004 Olympic Games.

Athletes Caught Taking Illegal Drugs
- Greek weight lifter Leonidas Sampanis won a bronze medal. Later he failed a drug test and was the first athlete in Athens to lose his medal.
- Russian shot-putter Irina Korzhanenko won a gold medal. Then she tested positive for steroids and had to give back the medal.
- A women's rowing team from the Ukraine won a bronze medal and lost it after Olena Olefirenko tested positive for a banned stimulant.
- Weight lifter Zoltan Kovacs of Hungary finished last. But he was asked to leave The Games because he refused to take a drug test. He was the tenth weight lifter punished for doping.
- Greek runners Kostas Kenteris and Katerina Thanou said that they missed a drug test because they were in a motorcycle accident. When the International Olympic Committee started investigating, they dropped out of the Olympics.
- Aleksey Lesnichyi, a high jumper from Belarus, left The Games after he tested positive for steroids.

- Colombian cyclist Maria Luisa Calle Williams lost her bronze medal after testing positive for a stimulant.
- The International Olympic Committee (IOC) did not allow Kenyan boxer David Munyasia to compete in the Olympics because he tested positive for a banned stimulant before The Games began.
- Puerto Rican wrestler Mabel Fonseca lost her fifth-place finish after testing positive for a banned steroid.
- The International Weightlifting Federation did not allow Wafa Ammouri of Morocco, Zoltan Kecskes of Hungary, Viktor Chislean of Moldova, Pratima Kumari Na of India, and Sule Sahbaz of Turkey to compete in the Olympics because they failed drug tests.
- Female weight lifters also had problems. Myanmar's Nan Aye Khine and India's Sanamacha Chanu both got fourth place in two different weight classes. However, they later tested positive for banned drugs. They had to leave the competition.
- Four days before the start of The Games, two Greek baseball players, a Swiss cyclist, a Spanish canoe team member, and an Irish distance runner were banned because of doping.
- American runner Torri Edwards was not allowed to compete because she tested positive for a stimulant at an April race prior to the Olympics.

Reading Comprehension

Check Your Predictions

1. Look back at questions 1–4 in the Predict section. How correct were your predictions?

Prediction	Correct	Not Correct
1		
2		
3		
4		

2. If you found the answers to your questions, what were they?

   Reading 1: _____

   Reading 2: _____

Check the Facts

A. Read the statements and write *true* (T) or *false* (F). Go back to Reading 1 and look for the answers you are unsure of.

_____ 1. More athletes are taking drugs than before.

_____ 2. Professional athletes don't take drugs.

_____ 3. Some athletes take drugs so they don't feel pain.

_____ 4. Athletes must take drug tests before they compete in the Olympics.

_____ 5. All drugs cause cancer.

B. Answer the questions.

1. What kinds of effects do drugs have?

   _____

2. According to the writer, why do athletes take drugs?

   _____

3. Why is winning important to athletes?

   _____

READING 2

A. Write the names of countries with athletes that were caught doping.

   _____

   _____

   _____

   _____

B. Write the names of sports with athletes that were caught doping.

   _____   _____   _____

   _____   _____   _____

   _____   _____   _____

C. Answer the questions.

1. What sport had the most athletes caught doping?
2. What were some of the punishments?

Analyze

Answer the questions. Give reasons for your answers.

1. What kinds of drugs do you think these different types of athletes might take?

   a. weight lifters _____

   b. runners _____

   c. cyclists _____

   d. wrestlers _____

2. Why did the writer of Reading 2 choose to name all of the offending athletes, their countries, and their sports?

Vocabulary Work

Guess Meaning from Context

1. What *world knowledge* may help you guess the meaning of the following informal phrases?

   a. the big game _____

   b. bragging rights _____

   c. talk big _____

2. Guess the meaning of these words from Reading 1. What clues did you use?

   a. mask _____

   b. banned _____

   c. restricted _____

   d. consequences _____

3. The writer in Reading 2 uses the word *banned* to describe two kinds of different things. What are they?

   _____

   _____

Guess Meaning from Related Words

1. The following words are in the readings. Find other words that are related to them.

    Reading 1

    compete   _____

    risks   _____

    advantage _____

    Reading 2

    Olympics   _____   _____
    (Note: One form is used as a noun and an adjective.)

2. Work in pairs. Draw a chart like this one in your notebook. Put the words from Exercise 1 in the correct columns. Compare your work with another pair when you are done.

Noun (person)	Noun (thing)	Verb	Adjective	Adverb

3. Find common words or parts of common words inside these nouns.

    a. weightlifting   _____

    b. motorcycle   _____

    c. unclean   _____

    d. baseball   _____

    e. teenagers   _____

Reading Skills

Using Charts

Writers use charts in a number of different ways:
- *to restate information in a different way*
- *to give an example*
- *to give extra information*

1. What is the main purpose of the chart in Reading 1?

    _____

2. Which part of the chart has the most helpful information?

    a. the names of the drugs

    b. the names of the types of drugs

    c. the use of each drug

Discussion

1. Do you think sports doping is a problem? Why or why not?
2. How often do you think professional athletes win because of drugs?

PART II

Read the next article to find the answers to these questions.

1. Why do some people think that sports doping is not a problem?
2. Why does the writer disagree with them?
3. How can sports doping get out of control?
4. What do some parents do about drugs?
5. According to the writer, what is the real problem?

The Real Danger of Sports Doping

Some people ask, "What's wrong with athletes using drugs to help them compete better?" They say, "Even if drugs are dangerous, the athletes choose to take the risk." In other words, athletes should have complete control over their own bodies. They have the right to use any drug they want.

There are several problems with this argument. However, the most important one is that doping creates an unfair <u>environment</u>. Imagine that you and I are runners. I take drugs to help me run faster and I win. You think that you must also take drugs to have a fair chance.

One can easily see how doping would soon get out of control. If *you* start doping, *I* have to find another way to keep my advantage. Perhaps, I will decide to take more drugs. Maybe I will look for different, stronger drugs to give me a better chance. If I do this, you must follow me or lose. Both of us would continue taking greater and greater risks.

Multiply this situation by thousands. Expand it from professional athletes to amateurs, including children. You may be thinking, "Children? Who lets their children take drugs?" We all know parents who want their children to win <u>at all costs</u>. For them, there is no coach that is too expensive; no amount of practice that is too much; no sacrifice that is too great. These parents let their children take drugs to improve their chances. After all, they might <u>win</u> a professional career, a college scholarship, or at least bragging rights for their proud parents.

In the end, of course, the real problem is not the doping. It is the win-at-all-costs attitude. The importance of winning in sports is more important than ever before. With the high value on winning, doping is unavoidable. We can ban drugs. We can test athletes. We can even stop them from competing, but we will never solve the problem until we change our attitudes.

Vocabulary Work

Guess Meaning from Context

1. Can you guess the meanings of these words and phrases? What clues did you use?

Words	Meaning
control	_____
out of control	_____
fair	_____
unfair	_____
professional	_____
amateur	_____

2. Look at the underlined words in the reading. How are the meanings different from the meanings that you know?

Reading Skills

Understanding the Use of Examples

Writers sometimes use an imaginary example to explain a point.

1. What imaginary example does this writer use?
2. What words does the writer use to show that the example is not real?
3. What important idea does this example support?
4. Is it an effective example? Why or why not?

Idea Exchange

Think about Your Ideas

Read the situations. Answer the questions. Explain your answers.

1. You are a high school football player. You work really hard and practice more than your friends, but you rarely play in games. The coach says that you run and catch the ball really well but you are too small. A friend says that you should take steroids. They will help you get bigger and no one tests for drugs at your school.

Would you agree to take the drug?   probably not   probably   sure

Why? _____

_____

2. You are an excellent athlete. You have a chance to represent your country in the Olympics. Your coach says that your competitors are using banned drugs. He thinks that you should use them, too. He says that there is one drug that they can't find in drug tests.

Would you agree to take the drug?   probably not   probably   sure

Why? _____

_____

3. You are a professional athlete. A clothing company wants you to advertise their sports clothes. They offer you a big contract if you win the championship. You might win and you might not. If you take a stimulant, you'll win for sure.

Would you take it?   probably not   probably   sure

Why? _____

_____

Talk about Your Ideas

Look at these two statements. Which do you agree with? Why?

1. *It's not whether you win or lose, it's how you play the game.*
   —Grantland Rice, American sports writer (1880–1954)

2. *Winning isn't everything. It's the only thing.*
   —Vince Lombardi, American football coach (1913–1970)

For CNN video activities about the scandal of drug use in sports, turn to page 177.

CHAPTER 10

WHITE-COLLAR CRIME: WHEN *A LOT* JUST ISN'T ENOUGH!

a.

b.

c.

PREVIEW

Answer the question.

Which of the people in these photographs are criminals?

(Answers are on the next page.)

PART I

Predict

A. Quickly skim these two articles. Circle the answers.

Which article . . .

1. talks about the topic in general?

   Reading 1   Reading 2   Readings 1 & 2

2. explains where the term *white-collar crime* comes from?

   Reading 1   Reading 2   Readings 1 & 2

3. explains different kinds of white-collar crime?

   Reading 1   Reading 2   Readings 1 & 2

4. gives reasons for this kind of crime?

   Reading 1   Reading 2   Readings 1 & 2

B. Write a question that you think each article will answer.

Reading 1: _____

Reading 2: _____

> Answer to Preview question: All of these people have been convicted of or are on trial for corporate crimes: (a) Dennis Kozlowski—on trial for grand larceny, securities fraud, falsifying business records; (b) Lea and Andrew Fastow—convicted of tax evasion, conspiracy, and fraud; (c) Martha Stewart—convicted of obstructing justice and lying to investigators.

Read It

Read the articles. Look for the answers to your questions.

 READING 1   What Is White-Collar Crime?

Sociologist Edwin Sutherland was the first person to use the term *white-collar crime.* Sutherland used the phrase *white-collar* because most of the criminals that he studied were white-collar workers—people with occupations that don't require manual labor. These included business people, government workers, doctors, and lawyers. He compared white-collar crime with street crime. In one basic way these criminals are the same—people commit these crimes for money. However, they are different in another important way. Street crime is often physically violent. White-collar criminals usually hurt people's finances, but they don't often hit them.

Before Sutherland, sociologists believed that poverty was the cause of most crime; they thought that people committed crimes because they were poor. Sutherland argued that wealthy people were often criminals, too. They weren't poor. They were just greedy. They were people who had a lot, but wanted more. Sutherland also believed that white-collar crime was more dangerous than street crime, even though it was nonviolent. Why? Because it made people distrust important social institutions such as government and business organizations.

The Federal Bureau of Investigation (FBI) says that white-collar crime costs the United States more than $300 billion every year. The punishment for white-collar crimes include fines, home detention, community confinement, costs of prosecution, forfeitures, restitution, supervised release, and imprisonment. However, it can be very difficult to catch white-collar criminals. They often cover their crimes in complex financial arrangements that are difficult to understand. For this reason, there is a new profession called *forensic accounting.* Forensic accountants look for evidence of crime in a company's finances.

 READING 2   White-Collar Criminals

What Do White-Collar Criminals Do?

White-collar criminals commit the following crimes:

- **Fraud:** Getting money by "selling" products or services that do not actually exist or that don't do what the criminals say they can.
- **Embezzlement:** Taking money or property that the white-collar criminal controls but does not own.
- **Bribery:** Giving a government worker or company employee a gift so that the person will help the criminal.
- **Forgery:** Signing another person's name to a check or other legal paper.
- **Insider Trading:** Using information that the public doesn't know in order to decide to buy or sell stock.

- **Kickback:** Similar to a **bribe.** Giving money back to the person who purchased your service or product; this money profits the buyer, not the buyer's business.
- **Money Laundering:** Investing money from an illegal business *(dirty money)* in a legal business to cover or hide criminal activity.

Why Do They Do It?

White-collar criminals do not look like criminals. They aren't poor. They don't associate with other criminals. They usually live ordinary lives and they are well respected at work and in their community. So why do they commit crimes?

- **Greed:** Even though they aren't poor, they want more money than they can earn legally.
- **Power:** They feel that money is power. They want to *win* at all costs.
- **Anger at The System:** Some white-collar criminals are angry at their companies, their bosses, or society.
- **Corporate Modeling:** Some corporations are not good role models. They teach their employees that lying or *stretching the truth* is acceptable. If the company doesn't act morally, their employees often feel that it's OK to cheat it.

What Happens to White-Collar Criminals?

White-collar criminals often are not punished because

- they have very high positions and a lot of power. People are afraid of them;
- there is a long history of small punishments for white-collar crime;
- many white-collar crimes seem victimless. People may not even realize that they are *victims.*

Reading Comprehension

Check Your Predictions

1. Look back at questions 1–4 in the Predict section. How correct were your predictions?

Prediction	Correct	Not Correct
1		
2		
3		
4		

2. If you found the answers to your questions, what were they?

Reading 1: _____

Reading 2: _____

Check the Facts

READING 1

A. **Read the statements and write** *true* **(T) or** *false* **(F). Go back to the reading and look for the answers you are unsure of.**

_____ 1. Edwin Sutherland studied white-collar crime.

_____ 2. People with high-level jobs usually wear white shirts.

_____ 3. White-collar criminals are often violent.

_____ 4. Sutherland believed that only high-class people are criminals.

_____ 5. White-collar criminals sometimes go to jail.

_____ 6. Forensic accountants help catch criminals.

B. **Answer the questions.**

1. What kind of people commit white-collar crime?

2. Which department of the U.S. government investigates white-collar crime?

READING 2

A. Read each situation and name the crime it describes.

_____ 1. A lawyer steals money from his client's account.

_____ 2. A teenager signs her mother's name to a check.

_____ 3. The manager of a company buys all his computers from one store. The store gives him ten percent of the price.

_____ 4. A man wins money from illegal gambling. He uses that money to buy stock.

_____ 5. You buy a camera on the Internet. The company sends you a different, less expensive camera.

_____ 6. Your neighbor gives a city official some money. Then your neighbor's company gets a contract to clean the roads in the city.

B. Answer the questions.

1. What are some of the reasons for white-collar crime?
2. How do white-collar criminals avoid punishment?

Analyze

Answer the questions. Give reasons for your answers.

1. Compare white-collar criminals to street criminals.
2. Which of these items might a white-collar criminal use?

   gun

   computer

   the Internet

   knife

   mask

   getaway car

   telephone

Vocabulary Work

Guess Meaning from Context

1. Guess the meaning of these words. What clues did you use?

   Reading 1

   social institutions _____

   greedy _____

   forensic accounting _____

   Reading 2

   property _____

   control _____

   associate _____

   greed _____

   stretching the truth _____

2. In Reading 1, there is a long list of unknown words:

   fines, home detention, community confinement, costs of prosecution, forfeitures, restitution, supervised release, and imprisonment

   Even if you do not understand any of these words, you can understand something about the list. What is it?

   a. The punishments for white-collar crime are very strong.

   b. There are many different kinds of punishments for white-collar crime.

   c. White-collar crime doesn't have strong punishments.

Guess Meaning from Related Words

1. The following words are in Reading 1. Find other words that are related to them.

   poor   _____

   violent _____

   crime   _____

   trust   _____

2. Work in pairs. Draw a chart like this one in your notebook. Put the words from Exercise 1 in the correct columns. Compare your work with another pair when you are done.

Noun (person)	Noun (thing)	Verb	Adjective	Adverb

3. Find common words or parts of common words inside these phrases.

   white-collar workers   _____

   well respected   _____

   victimless   _____

Reading Skills

Finding Referents

What does each <u>underlined</u> word or phrase refer to? (Note that one word has no referent.)

. . . most of the criminals that he studied were white-collar workers—people with occupations that don't require manual labor. <u>These</u> included business people, government workers, doctors, and lawyers. He compared white-collar crime with street crime. In one basic way <u>they</u> are the same—

people commit these crimes for money. However, they are different in another important way. Street crime is often physically violent. White-collar criminals usually hurt people's finances, but they don't often hit them.
3   4

Before Sutherland, sociologists believed that poverty was the cause of most crime. They thought that people committed crimes because they
5   6
were poor. Sutherland argued that wealthy people were often criminals, too. They weren't poor. They were just greedy. They were people who
7
had a lot, but wanted more. Sutherland also believed that white-collar crime was more dangerous than street crime, even though it was nonviolent.
8
Why? Because it made people distrust important social institutions
9
such as government and business organizations.

The Federal Bureau of Investigation (FBI) says that white-collar crime costs the United States more than $300 billion every year. The punishment for white-collar crimes include fines, home detention, community confinement, costs of prosecution, forfeitures, restitution, supervised release, and imprisonment. However, it can be very difficult to catch
10
white-collar criminals. They often cover their crimes in complex
11
financial arrangements that are difficult to understand. For this reason,
12
there is a new profession called *forensic accounting*. Forensic accountants look for evidence of crime in a company's financial records.

1. _____   7. _____

2. _____   8. _____

3. _____   9. _____

4. _____   10. _____

5. _____   11. _____

6. _____   12. _____

Discussion

1. Do you agree with Sutherland that white-collar crime is more dangerous to society than street crime?

2. Which types of white-collar crimes do you think are the most frequent?

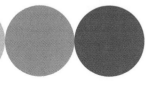

PART II

Read to find the answers.

1. Why did Martha Stewart go to jail?

2. Who is Laura Nash?

3. What did Dennis Kozlowski do?

4. What are some of the characteristics of business superstars?

5. What advice does Nash have for business people?

 (READING)   ## Why an Awful Lot Sometimes Just Isn't Enough

Martha Stewart was incredibly successful. She was the head of her own corporation and one of the richest women in the United States. In 2004, she went to jail for *insider trading.* Stewart used *inside information* to avoid losing $50,000. That's a lot of money to most people, but Stewart was a billionaire. So, why did she do it?

Laura Nash teaches business at Harvard University. She says that Stewart had one problem—she was greedy. "The definition of success today is to go for the maximum. That gets people in trouble." Nash said Stewart and many other business executives are addicted to making money. They don't know when to stop.

Dennis Kozlowski is another great example of a greedy millionaire. He was the head of Tyco International, and his salary was more than $100 million a year. Apparently it wasn't enough, so he *borrowed* millions of dollars more from the company. Then he used this money to buy antiques, art, and furniture for his New York apartment. The company also <u>lent</u> him $19 million to pay for a home in Florida. In 2002, Tyco paid for half of the cost of his wife's birthday party in Italy. (It cost $2.1 million.) The problem with the *loans* was that the company forgave them—they didn't ask him to repay the money. Then they *forgot* to tell the company's stockholders about these *gifts*. In 2004, the police arrested Kozlowski for stealing about $135 million from the company.

According to Nash, people like Stewart and Kozlowski are business superstars. They are as famous as rock stars and even richer. They often get *drunk* on success. People like this can be very selfish and self-centered. Most importantly, they don't think that they have to *play by the rules*. Nash believes that business leaders who are not so famous do better. They often have lasting success over a lifetime. They know how to deal with disappointment and limitations. In general, they also care more about others and share their wealth.

Many business superstars believe they can have it all. "Martha Stewart thought she could be the happiest, most caring, wealthiest person around," Nash said. "Nobody can be all of those things." Stewart's fall is a valuable lesson for managers, she said. "To have real success, you must stay true to your values. You have to be able to say, 'This is enough.'"

Vocabulary Work

Understanding Words in Italics

Writers use italics to show that he or she is using a word or phrase in a different way from the usual. Look at each of the phrases in italics. Explain how their meanings are different from normal.

1. Stewart used *inside information* to avoid losing $50,000.

2. Apparently it wasn't enough, so he *borrowed* millions of dollars more from the company.

3. The company also *lent* him $19 million to pay for a home in Florida.

4. The problem with the *loans* was that the company forgave them—they didn't ask him to repay the money.

5. Then they *forgot* to tell the company's stockholders about these *gifts*.

6. They often get *drunk* on success.

7. Most importantly, they don't think that they have to *play by the rules*.

Reading Skills

Finding Referents

What does each <u>underlined</u> word or phrase refer to? Look back to the reading if necessary.

1. <u>That's</u> a lot of money to most people, but Stewart was a billionaire.
2. So, why did she do <u>it</u>?
3. <u>That</u> gets people in trouble.
4. <u>They</u> don't know when to stop.
5. Apparently <u>it</u> wasn't enough, so he *borrowed* millions of dollars more from the company.
6. Then he used <u>this money</u> to buy antiques, art, and furniture for his New York apartment.
7. <u>It</u> cost $2.1 million.
8. The problem with the *loans* was that the company forgave <u>them</u>.
9. <u>They</u> didn't ask him to repay the money.
10. People like <u>this</u> can be very selfish and self-centered.
11. Nobody can be all of <u>those things</u>.
12. <u>This</u> is enough.

Idea Exchange

Think about Your Ideas

Answer this questionnaire.

Would you ever . . .	Never	Probably not	Maybe	Sure
1. cheat on your taxes?				
2. sell a car with a serious problem and not tell the buyer?				
3. take something from your employer worth less than $25?				
4. take something from your employer worth more than $100?				
5. *borrow* money from your child's bank account?				
6. pay a police officer to *fix* a traffic ticket?				

Talk about Your Ideas

1. How big a problem is white-collar crime?
2. Do you agree that all of the activities in the questionnaire are crimes? Why or why not?
3. Should white-collar criminals go to jail like street criminals?

For CNN video activities about white-collar crime, turn to page 178.

CHAPTER 11

THE HOMELESS:
IT'S NOT THEIR CHOICE

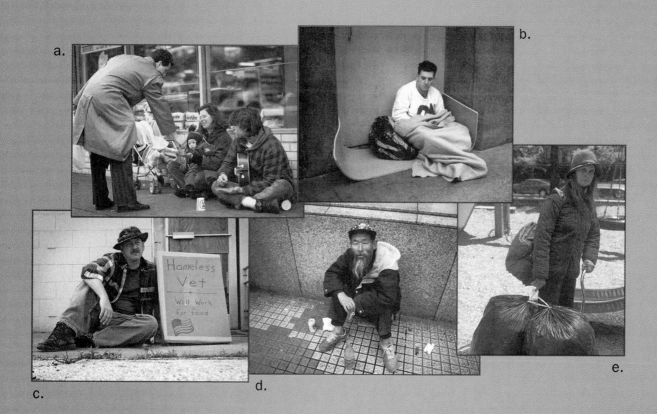

a.

b.

c.

d.

e.

Homeless
Vet

Will Work
for food

PREVIEW

Discuss the answers to these questions.

1. Look at the photographs. Who looks homeless? Who would you give money to?

2. In the United States, many people say the following things about the homeless. Are these statements true or false in your opinion?

_____ a. They prefer to live on the street.

_____ b. It's their fault that they are homeless.

_____ c. They don't work.

_____ d. They are mentally ill.

_____ e. They are drug addicts.

_____ f. They are dangerous.

Internet information: Go to http://elt.thomson.com/hottopics/ for more information about the homeless in the United States.

3. Do people have the same opinions about the homeless in other countries?

PART 1

Predict

A. Quickly skim these two articles. Circle the answers.

Which article . . .

1. is a movie review?

    Reading 1   Reading 2   Readings 1 & 2

2. gives the writer's opinion about homeless people?

    Reading 1   Reading 2   Readings 1 & 2

3. has statistics?

    Reading 1   Reading 2   Readings 1 & 2

4. gives a problem and a solution?

    Reading 1   Reading 2   Readings 1 & 2

B. Write a question that you think each article will answer.

Reading 1: _____

Reading 2: _____

Read It

Read the articles. Look for the answers to your questions.

 (READING 1)

Homeless to Harvard

Film: *Homeless to Harvard: The Liz Murray Story*
Genre: Drama
Directed by: Peter Levin
Produced by: Michael Mahoney
Starring: Thora Birch, Kelly Lynch, Michael Riley, Robert Bockstael, Aron Tager

The Story

Homeless to Harvard is the amazing true story of Liz Murray. Liz grew up in very difficult circumstances. Her parents were drug addicts. They didn't have jobs. The family got a check from the government every month. However, her parents used a lot of the money to buy drugs. Therefore, they often did not have enough to eat. Liz's parents finally divorced. When she was 15, her mother died from AIDS.

Liz's father was living in a homeless shelter, so she couldn't live with him. She refused to go into the child welfare system because she didn't want to live with strangers in a foster family or a group home. Liz and her friend started living on the streets of New York City.

The girls' lives were incredibly difficult. In good weather, they slept in public parks. In bad weather, they slept underground on the subway. They just rode the trains all night. They ate from garbage cans and asked strangers for money. At the same time, Liz realized that another life was possible. She used a friend's address and started classes in a public high school. She took double the normal number of classes, so she finished in two years. During this time, Liz's class took a trip to Harvard University and she decided that she wanted to go there. She eventually earned a scholarship and, in 2000, she entered Harvard.

My Opinion ★★✦

The best thing about *Homeless to Harvard* is that it is a true story. This movie teaches us many lessons about hope and a person's ability to succeed despite difficulties. Thora Birch does a good job as Liz. But the direction is not strong. It's a movie you can see once but no more.

 **READING 2**   The Working Poor

Most people do not know that many of the homeless have jobs. They just don't make enough money to pay rent. In Washington, D.C., minimum wage is $5.25 an hour. A one-bedroom apartment costs about $500 a week. Therefore, a person would have to work 92 hours a week to pay the rent. However, there are only 168 hours in a week, so this is obviously impossible.

A major difficulty is that there is not enough affordable or inexpensive housing available. The government says that no household should pay more than 30 percent of its income for rent. However, today more than 5.4 million families pay more than 50 percent of their income for rent. In 1995, there were 4.4 million more low-income renters than there were affordable housing units. Unfortunately, the situation is getting worse. Government policies are making more and more people homeless.

The government doesn't help the *working poor.* If their income is above $8,277 annually, they cannot receive money from the government. However, that amount of money may not be enough to pay rent. A typical working family with children and no government help can use up their monthly income in two days. How is that possible? Think about car payments, insurance, baby diapers, and food.

Many of the working poor are very close to becoming homeless. They usually live from paycheck to paycheck. They can't save anything. Therefore, any extra expense is a major problem. If the car breaks down or someone gets sick, there may not be enough money for rent. If they cannot pay rent, they will soon be out on the street.

Reading Comprehension

Check Your Predictions

1. Look back at questions 1–4 in the Predict section. How correct were your predictions?

Prediction	Correct	Not Correct
1		
2		
3		
4		

2. If you found the answers to your questions, what were they?

Reading 1: _____

Reading 2: _____

Check the Facts

READING 1

A. Read the statements and write *true* (T) or *false* (F). Go back to Reading 1 and look for the answers you are unsure of.

_____ 1. *Homeless to Harvard* is a movie.

_____ 2. Liz Murray was a drug addict.

_____ 3. Her mother died when she was a teenager.

_____ 4. Liz went to live with her father.

_____ 5. Liz finished high school.

_____ 6. Thora Birch wrote *Homeless to Harvard*.

B. Answer the questions.

1. How did Liz's family get money?

2. Where did Liz and her friend live?

3. How did Liz and her friend get money?

READING 2

A. Read the statements and write *true* (T) or *false* (F). Go back to Reading 2 and look for the answers you are unsure of.

_____ 1. Many homeless people have jobs.

_____ 2. Affordable housing is not expensive.

_____ 3. There is too much affordable housing available.

_____ 4. Families that make less than $8,277 get government help.

_____ 5. The working poor are always homeless.

B. Find the numbers in the reading.

1. The minimum wage: _____

2. The cost of a one-bedroom apartment in Washington, D.C.: _____

3. The total number of hours in a week: _____

4. The percentage of income families should pay for rent: _____

5. The percentage of income many poor families pay for rent: _____

Analyze

Answer the questions. Give reasons for your answers.

1. How was Liz Murray's family situation similar to the working poor in Reading 2?

2. How was it different?

Vocabulary Work

Guess Meaning from Context

1. You can use your knowledge of organization to help you. The first sentence in a paragraph often gives the main idea. If you do not understand all the words in this sentence, the rest of the paragraph may help you.

How does the paragraph explain the word *circumstances?*

> Liz grew up in very difficult circumstances. Her parents were drug addicts. They didn't have jobs. The family got a check from the government every month. However, her parents used a lot of the money to buy drugs. Therefore, they often did not have enough to eat. Liz's parents finally divorced. When she was 15, her mother died from AIDS.

2. Use your *world knowledge* and the context to help you guess the approximate meaning of the underlined words.

> Liz's father was living in a <u>homeless shelter</u>, so she couldn't live with him. She refused to go into the <u>child welfare system</u> because she didn't want to live with strangers in a <u>foster family</u> or a <u>group home</u>.

3. An example can also help you understand meaning.

> Therefore, any <u>extra expense</u> is a major problem. If the car breaks down or someone gets sick, there may not be enough money for rent.

4. Can you guess the meaning of these idioms?
   - live from paycheck to paycheck: _____
   - out on the street: _____

Guess Mean from Related Words

1. Find common words or parts of common words inside these compound words.

   paycheck   _____

   subway   _____

   underground   _____

2. Guess the meaning of these phrases.

   public parks   _____

   garbage cans   _____

3. Sometimes a writer can use *the* + an adjective to refer to a group of people—for example, *the homeless.* Find another example in Reading 2.

Reading Skills

Understanding Transition Words

1. In the paragraph below, match the <u>underlined</u> transition words with their functions.

   a. to introduce an opposite idea

   b. to give a result

   c. to give a reason

<u>However</u>, her parents used a lot of the money to buy drugs. <u>Therefore</u>, they often did not have enough to eat. Liz's parents finally divorced. When she was 15, her mother died from AIDS. Liz's father was living in a homeless shelter, <u>so</u> she couldn't live with him.

1. _____
2. _____
3. _____

2. Scan Reading 2 for places where the writer uses *however, so,* and *therefore.*

Discussion

1. Is homelessness a problem in your native country? Why or why not?
2. Should the government help the homeless? If so, what kind of help should it give them?

PART II

Read to find the answers to these questions.

1. Where is this reading probably from? Who wrote it?
2. What are police in San Miguel doing?
3. What is the writer's opinion?
4. What does the writer want the city to do?

 READING

Let's Help, Not Hurt the Homeless

The city of San Miguel should be ashamed of itself. Police are now giving tickets for "illegal lodging" to people who sleep outside. Like most cities in the United States, San Miguel does not have enough affordable housing or homeless shelters. Today, the city only has 2,734 emergency and shelter beds. This number is not nearly enough for the 8,000 homeless who sleep outside every night.

City officials have created a different solution to the problem.

They are punishing people for being homeless. They are giving them tickets that they can't pay. Sometimes they even arrest them and take them to jail. They are actually criminalizing homelessness. In 2000, homeless people received 516 tickets in eight districts in the city. From January 2003 through March 2004, police gave out 2,641 tickets in just two districts. Interestingly, these are the two districts right next to the new baseball park.

These actions are not just an embarrassment; they are probably not legal. The United States signed the Universal Declaration of Human Rights in 1948. Perhaps the mayor and other city officials should read it. It says, "Everyone has the right to a standard of living adequate for the health and well-being of himself and of his family, including food, clothing, housing and medical care, and necessary social services."

No one likes to see the homeless on the street. However, we shouldn't punish people because they have no place to live. We should help them find homes. We ask city officials to focus on positive solutions—increased housing and services that will help people get off the street. These people need a helping hand, not a slap across the face.

—The Editor

Vocabulary Work

Guess Meaning from Context

1. Can you guess the meanings of these words? What clues did you use?

   Clues: a. It looks like a word I know.

         b. It has an example.

         c. I used world knowledge.

   illegal   _____

   criminalizing   _____

   interestingly   _____

   embarrassment   _____

   standard of living   _____

   mayor   _____

   well-being   _____

2. What clues help you guess the meaning of *a slap across the face*?

Reading Skills

Identifying the Author's Purpose

1. Is the writer trying to persuade, explain, describe, or teach his audience?

2. Find words or phrases to support your answer.

Analyzing an Argument

1. When you read an opinion, it is important to look carefully at the details that the writer uses to support his or her argument. Which of these details did this writer use?

   a. statistics
   b. other types of facts
   c. quotations
   d. examples
   e. personal experience

2. What important idea does each detail support?

3. Did the writer make a good argument? Why or why not?

Idea Exchange

Think about Your Ideas

Read these three situations. Circle the type of help you think each person should get.

A. My name is Maggie. I am 28 years old and I have two children. Sammy is six and Greta is three. We used to live with my boyfriend, Rick. He is Greta's father. He lost his job at the furniture factory and started drinking. When he got drunk, he got really violent and hit me. Finally, I took the children and left. We drove 600 miles to the city where I used to live. I couldn't find any of my old friends. We're living in my car. I can't get a job because I have no child care.

1. Take the children from their mother and put them in foster care.

2. Give the family an apartment and find a job for the mother and child care for the children.

3. Help the mother contact her family.

4. Find the father and make him give his family money.

5. Other: _____

B. I am 15 years old. My name is Angela. I ran away from home because of my stepfather. He and I fought constantly. He used to hit me and punish me all the time. My mother tried to stop him, but he didn't listen. Four months ago, I stole some money from him and bought a bus ticket. Life on the streets is hard. My money ran out a long time ago. At first, I begged for money in the bus station, but I couldn't make enough money that way. Now I work for a drug dealer. I have no choice. If I don't sell drugs, I'll have to sell myself. I can't ask anyone for help because they'll send me home.

1. Put Angela in a foster home.
2. Put her in a group home with other teenagers.
3. Send her home if her parents go to a counselor.
4. Send her home immediately.
5. Other: _____

C. I'm Rick. I am 35 years old. I lost my job as a bus driver because I kept missing work. I suffer from depression. Some days I cannot get out of bed. There are drugs for my problem, but I can't afford them. I owe my landlord two months rent. If I don't pay him, he'll kick me out. I don't know what to do. My ex-wife and my kids live in Florida, but I can't ask them for help.

1. Make him ask his ex-wife and children for help.
2. Pay for his drugs so that he can go to work.
3. Make him live in a group home for the mentally ill.
4. Give him money so that he does not have to work.
5. Other: _____

Talk about Your Ideas

In groups, discuss the three situations. How are they similar? How are they different? Does each person deserve the same amount of help? Why or why not?

For CNN video activities about the homeless, turn to page 179.

CHAPTER 12

Beauty Contests:
The business of beauty

PREVIEW

Discuss the answers to these questions.

1. What beauty contests do you know about?

2. Are there beauty contests in your country? If so, who competes?

3. Do you know anyone who has ever been in a beauty contest? What happened?

PART I

Predict

A. Quickly skim these two articles. Circle the answers.

Which article . . .

1. discusses beauty contests for real people?

   Reading 1   Reading 2   Readings 1 & 2

2. reports on an unusual beauty contest?

   Reading 1   Reading 2   Readings 1 & 2

3. gives two sides of a story?

   Reading 1   Reading 2   Readings 1 & 2

4. gives the author's opinion?

   Reading 1   Reading 2   Readings 1 & 2

B. Write a question that you think each article will answer.

Reading 1: _____

Reading 2: _____

Read It

Read the articles. Look for the answers to your questions.

 READING 1   Pretty Babies

    Tina Crosby looked confused. This was her first beauty contest and she was nervous. The judge asked her, "How do you relax?" She bravely tried to smile, but she couldn't answer the question. "Ummm. I don't know," was all that she could say.

    That's not surprising. Tina is only five years old. She was not well-spoken but she was cute enough to win. A smiling Tina (and her proud mother) went home with a trophy and a "diamond" crown.

    Beauty contests for very young children are common today. However, many people are asking, "Are they good for children?" Megan Palmer runs

children's beauty pageants. She knows that there can be problems. She says that some parents push their children too hard. She once saw a woman hit her child. The mother was angry because the girl did not walk gracefully enough. And she says that some mothers put too much makeup on their daughter's faces. "The girls look 30 years old. I tell the mothers to calm down. Then I give them soap and a washcloth and tell them to wash it off," she says.

Palmer also does not like professional coaches. Some parents pay thousands of dollars for lessons. They want their daughters to learn to walk, turn, and wave to the audience correctly. In addition, the coaches tell the girls how to answer questions as Palmer explains. "For example, a judge asks, 'What would you like to be when you grow up?' the five-year-old then answers, 'I want to be a history teacher and president of the United States.' That wasn't the child's answer. It was the coach's answer."

Palmer tries to make sure that the children are enjoying themselves. "Beauty contests," she says, "should be fun. They also should help children become more self-confident—being in a beauty contest is the same as playing on a soccer team. It's not about winning."

Many experts do not agree. Some child psychologists say that the contests have many more disadvantages than advantages. They think that they teach girls that beauty is very important. Others worry that these children grow up too fast and that can cause psychological problems later on.

Unfortunately for the girls, baby beauty contests are big business. Ted Cohen publishes the International Directory of Pageants. He says there are probably about 5,000 beauty pageants in the United States every year. About 25 percent are for children. And the business is growing. There are more and more contests every year.

READING 2   The Search for an Internet Beauty Queen

There's a new beauty contest for women—"virtual" women that is. *Miss Digital World* is the first beauty contest for video-game heroines such as Lara Croft. The contest is really for digital artists, advertising agencies, and video-game programmers. They are sending the computer design of their perfect woman to an Internet site.

The organizers want people to be serious about the contest. Each contestant must send in the following items and information:

- five photos
- date of birth, name, address, etc.
- hair color
- eye color
- height and other vital statistics
- video

And just like Miss America and Miss Universe, Miss Digital World must be a role model. No strippers or pornographic movie stars are allowed.

"Every age has its ideal of beauty—the Venus de Milo in ancient Greece and Marilyn Monroe in the 1960s," said Franz Cerami, the creator of the competition. Designers must make their "contestants" walk along a virtual catwalk. The digital woman who receives the most votes from Internet users will win. There will be a virtual presenter and virtual guests at the presentation. Cerami hopes the digital queen will be used in video games, advertisements, and films such as the *Matrix.*

Reading Comprehension

Check Your Predictions

1. Look back at questions 1–4 in the Predict section. How correct were your predictions?

Prediction	Correct	Not Correct
1		
2		
3		
4		

2. If you found the answers to your questions, what were they?

Reading 1: _____

Reading 2: _____

Check the Facts

READING 1

A. Read the statements and write *true* (T) or *false* (F). Go back to Reading 1 and look for the answers you are unsure of.

_____ 1. Tina Crosby won the beauty contest.

_____ 2. Megan Palmer judges children's beauty contests.

_____ 3. Megan Palmer says that parents sometimes push their children too hard.

_____ 4. Professional coaches work for free.

_____ 5. Palmer thinks that beauty contests are always fun.

_____ 6. Psychologists say that beauty contests have many advantages.

_____ 7. There are 5,000 children's beauty contests each year.

B. Answer the questions.

1. The writer mentions several people. What is each person's position?

Tina Crosby: _____

Megan Palmer: _____

Ted Cohen: _____

2. Summarize what each person says about beauty contests.

Megan Palmer: _____

_____

Psychologists: _____

_____

Ted Cohen: _____

_____

READING 2

A. Read the statements and write *true* (T) or *false* (F). Go back to Reading 2 and look for the answers you are unsure of.

_____ 1. *Miss Digital World* is an old competition.

_____ 2. The character of Lara Croft is a virtual woman.

_____ 3. Computer programmers create virtual characters.

_____ 4. Franz Cerami will decide the winner of the competition.

_____ 5. Miss Digital World must be a "good" woman.

_____ 6. In ancient Greece, people thought the Venus de Milo was the most perfect woman.

B. Answer the questions.

1. How is *Miss Digital World* similar to a normal beauty pageant?

_____

_____

2. How is *Miss Digital World* different from a normal beauty pageant?

_____

_____

Analyze

Answer the questions. Give reasons for your answers.

1. How might the *Miss Digital World* competition affect young girls?
2. What is strange about some of the information that *Miss Digital World* contestants have to send in?
3. Why do you think Cerami wants the winner of *Miss Digital World* to be a good role model?

Vocabulary Work

Guess Meaning from Context

1. What different types of *world knowledge* would help you guess the meaning of these words?

   cute   _____

   trophy   _____

   crown   _____

   wave   _____

   audience   _____

   vital statistics _____

   catwalk   _____

   virtual   _____

   digital   _____

2. Sometimes you can guess the meaning of a two-word verb if you just understand the first word. Guess the meaning of these words.

   calm down   _____

   wash off   _____

3. Can you guess the meaning of these words and phrases? What clues did you use?

   push . . . too hard _____

   makeup   _____

   big business   _____

   heroines   _____

Guess Meaning from Related Words

1. The following words are in the readings. Find other words that are related to them.

   Reading 1

   advantages _____

   psychological _____

   Reading 2

   contest _____

   presenter _____

2. Work in pairs. Draw a chart like this one in your notes. Put the words from Exercise 1 in the correct columns. Compare your work with another pair when you are done.

Noun (person)	Noun (thing)	Verb	Adjective	Adverb

3. Look at these hyphenated words. What do they mean?

   well-spoken _____

   self-confident _____

Reading Skills

Understanding Organization

The first paragraph of an article often introduces the subject of the article. It briefly tells the reader what the article is going to be about. However, a writer may start with a specific example rather than a general statement. This is particularly true in newspaper human-interest stories.

1. Look at Readings 1 and 2. Which one starts with a general introduction? Which one does not? What does it start with?

2. How does each introduction relate to the rest of the article? Does it help you understand the article? Why or why not?

Discussion

1. Palmer says, "Being in a beauty contest is the same as playing on a soccer team. It's not about winning." Do you agree or disagree? Why?

2. Why do you think parents enter their children in beauty contests?

3. Do you think the idea of a Miss Digital World is useful? Why or why not?

PART II

Read the next article to find the answers to these questions.

1. Are there beauty contests for men in the West? If so, what are they?

2. How do men win these contests?

3. What is important in a Wodaabe beauty contest?

4. What makes a Wodaabe man beautiful?

5. What do the Wodaabe men win?

Male Beauty

Beauty contests for women are very common. However, most men do not usually have opportunities to win prizes for being handsome. That is because most cultures don't consider a man's appearance as important as a woman's. Men don't have to be handsome, but women are supposed to be beautiful. However, there is one exception—bodybuilding.

In bodybuilding contests, men compete for cash prizes and titles such as Mr. Universe and Mr. America. The contestants stand in front of the judges and the audience. In order to show their muscles, they pose, or stand, in certain ways. There are competitions for separate parts of the body. One man might have the best back. Another might have the best chest or arms. However, there is also a prize for the best body overall. This man becomes Mr. Universe or Mr. America.

In a few other cultures there are also competitions for physical beauty for men. One interesting contest takes place in the Wodaabe culture. The Wodaabe live on the edge of the Sahara Desert in Africa. For the Wodaabe men, strength is not as important as beauty.

"It is our tradition. Even our ancestors are handsome. Our women are very beautiful, and the babies they make are the most beautiful," says Derre Chafou. He is a past winner. His father was also famous for his beauty. "If I am the man who is the prettiest, lots of women will want to marry me," Chafou explains.

The competition starts early in life. Mothers and sisters stretch the arms and legs of baby boys to make them long and thin. They squeeze their noses to make them pointed. Competitors' families may spend a year making their costumes. The young men sometimes travel for days to find the right clay to make their red-and-yellow face paint. And a competitor must be more than just beautiful to win. He must have *togu*—personal magnetism.

Magic also plays a big part in the competition. "Men try for ten years to get the right magic," Chafou explains. "Here all the men are beautiful. It's the power of magic that makes the difference."

In the end, there is no money, no crown, no trophy, no title. The most beautiful men win the right to marry the most beautiful women in the tribe so that they can make beautiful babies.

Vocabulary Work

Guess Meaning from Context

Can you guess the meanings of these words? What clues did you use?

1. appearance _____

2. bodybuilding _____

3. pose _____

4. overall _____

5. strength _____

6. magnetism _____

Reading Skills

Summarizing

1. When you summarize a reading, you use only the important points. You leave out the details. Read this summary of the first part of Reading 2.

   > Beauty contests for men are not common. One exception is bodybuilding. In this type of competition, men pose to show their muscles. The man with the best muscles wins the contest. He usually wins money and a title.

2. Now make a list of the important points about the Wodaabe beauty contest. First, answer the questions. Then write a short paragraph in your notebook.

   a. Who competes? _____

   b. How do they win? _____

   c. What do they win? _____

Idea Exchange

Think about Your Ideas

Which statements are true for you?

1. I would be in a beauty contest.
2. I would be a judge in a beauty contest.
3. I watch beauty contests on television.
4. I attend beauty contests.
5. I would encourage a friend to be in a beauty contest.
6. I would let my daughter be in a beauty contest.
7. I would protest against a beauty contest.

Talk about Your Ideas

Should there be beauty contests for women? For men? For children?
Why or why not?

**For CNN video activities about child beauty contests, turn
to page 180.**

CHAPTER 13

Drug Trends:
Legal but lethal

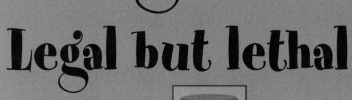

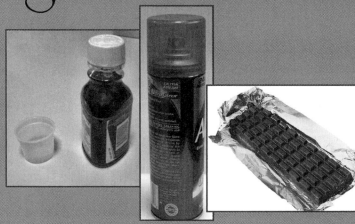

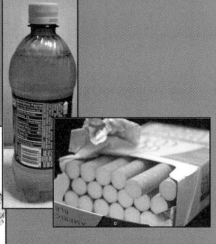

PREVIEW

Discuss the answers to these questions.

1. Which of these products contain something that might hurt you?

   a. soda

   b. cigarettes

   c. chocolate

   d. deodorant spray can

   e. cold medicine

   (Answer on next page)

2. What substances do they contain? How can each one hurt you?

PART I

Predict

A. Quickly skim these two articles. Circle the answers.

Which article . . .

1. discusses many drugs?

   Reading 1   Reading 2   Readings 1 & 2

2. talks about drugs in the past?

   Reading 1   Reading 2   Readings 1 & 2

3. tries to persuade people there is a problem?

   Reading 1   Reading 2   Readings 1 & 2

4. focuses on one age group?

   Reading 1   Reading 2   Readings 1 & 2

B. Write a question that you think each article will answer.

Reading 1: _____

Reading 2: _____

> Answer to Preview question 1: All of them

Read It

Read the articles. Look for the answers to your questions.

 (**READING 1**)   Cocaine: The Nineteenth Century
                                        Miracle Drug

   Long ago, Incas in South America discovered coca. Coca is a plant that contains a very powerful chemical—a drug. The Incas chewed coca leaves for energy. The Spanish conquistadors learned about coca, too. They took coca plants to Europe. There, in 1859, a German scientist learned how to take the drug out of the leaves. He called the drug *cocaine.*

Cocaine immediately became very popular. People thought it was a wonder drug. You could buy products with cocaine everywhere. Until 1914, you could buy it at department stores in the United States. There were cocaine medicines and even chocolate cocaine tablets. One popular drink was Vin Coca—coca wine. It contained 7.2 mg of cocaine per ounce of wine. In the 1880s, the psychiatrist Sigmund Freud said that cocaine was useful. He believed it cured depression and alcoholism.

One hundred years ago, cocaine was also an ingredient in the world's most famous soft drink—Coca Cola. At that time, it was a medicinal drink. It was named for its two main ingredients—coca leaves and kola nuts. People believed that Coca-Cola was beneficial; it made them feel better and more awake. That's not surprising. It contained cocaine from coca leaves and caffeine from kola nuts. Coca-Cola hasn't been made with cocaine for over 75 years.

Despite its benefits, cocaine wasn't popular for very long. People soon discovered that it wasn't really wonderful. Doctors saw that people quickly became dependent on the drug; they couldn't live without it. It also made some people a little crazy. Still others died from cocaine poisoning—they took too much of it. By the beginning of the twentieth century, companies were taking cocaine out of their products. Soon governments around the world made it illegal. Today cocaine is considered one of the most dangerous drugs.

 READING 2   Legal Drugs and Teenagers

A drug is any substance that changes the way the mind and body work. Some drugs—such as alcohol—are legal, while others—such as heroin, ecstasy, cannabis, cocaine, and LSD—are illegal. Still others—such as inhalants—have both legal and illegal uses.

Tobacco
Tobacco is the most common and dangerous legal drug. Long-term use causes serious diseases such as emphysema, heart disease, and lung cancer. In most places in the United States, you must be 18 to buy tobacco

products such as cigarettes, cigars, and chewing tobacco. However, studies show that almost 25 percent of young teenagers smoke regularly. In addition, 85 percent of teenagers who smoke become addicted.

Alcohol

Alcohol is a depressant that can affect people in many different ways. Some people are relaxed by the drug. Others lose their inhibitions completely so they do stupid, and sometimes dangerous, things. Some people become alcoholics. Alcoholics are people who are addicted to alcohol. Alcohol addiction destroys the lives of millions of people every year. Even though alcohol is legal for adults, it is illegal for teenagers. However, teenagers are drinking more than ever. Studies show that a third of American teenagers between the ages of 13 and 17 drink at least once a week. Many of them drink alcoholic fruit drinks. These sweet drinks often have more alcohol than beer or wine.

Inhalants

Inhalants are drugs that you can inhale or breathe in and get *high*. Inhaling, or *sniffing*, is very popular with very young teenagers because the products are easy to find. They are also inexpensive. Common household products such as glues, nail polish remover, lighter fluid, spray paints, deodorant, hair sprays, and cleaning fluids are *sniffable*. Most sniffers give up inhalants and start using alcohol or other drugs when they have more money. Inhalants can cause brain damage and even death.

Reading Comprehension

Check Your Predictions

1. Look back at questions 1–4 in the Predict section. How correct were your predictions?

Prediction	Correct	Not correct
1		
2		
3		
4		

2. If you found the answers to your questions, what were they?

Reading 1: _____

Reading 2: _____

Check the Facts

READING 1

A. Read the statements and write *true* (T) or *false* (F). Go back to Reading 1 and look for the answers you are unsure of.

_____ 1. The Incas knew how to make cocaine.

_____ 2. Coca leaves make you sleepy.

_____ 3. People used to believe that cocaine was not dangerous.

_____ 4. Freud knew that cocaine was bad.

_____ 5. Coca-Cola was made from coca leaves and kola nuts.

_____ 6. Farmers used cocaine to grow food.

_____ 7. Cocaine was popular for about 50 years.

B. Answer the questions.

1. How did cocaine make people feel?

2. What are some of the bad effects of cocaine?

READING 2

A. Read the statements and write true (T) or false (F). Go back to Reading 2 and look for the answers you are unsure of.

_____ 1. All drugs are illegal.

_____ 2. Anyone can buy cigarettes in the United States.

_____ 3. Tobacco can cause cancer.

_____ 4. Most teenagers who smoke become addicted to tobacco.

_____ 5. Alcohol is very dangerous for everyone.

_____ 6. Teenagers don't drink because it's illegal.

_____ 7. Teenagers prefer sweet drinks.

_____ 8. You can't drink an inhalant.

_____ 9. Anyone can buy an inhalant.

B. Complete the chart about the drugs discussed in Reading 2.

Type of Drug	Legal Use	Illegal Use	Effects

Analyze

Compare each of these drugs today to the situation with cocaine in 1880.

1. tobacco _____

2. alcohol _____

3. inhalants _____

Vocabulary Work

Guess Meaning from Context

When an unknown word names a category in a list, the items in the list can help you guess the meaning. Even if you do not know tobacco products, *cigarettes and* cigars *will help you guess its meaning:*

> . . . tobacco products such as cigarettes, cigars, and chewing tobacco. When an unknown word is part of the list, the other items in the list can also help you guess a general meaning. You may not know *chewing tobacco*, but you can guess that it is a tobacco product.

Now guess the meaning of the underlined phrases.

> Common household products such as glues, nail polish remover, lighter fluid, spray paints, deodorant, hair sprays, and cleaning fluids are *sniffable*.

Find the lists these words appear in to guess their meanings.

    a. depression _____

    b. cannabis _____

    c. emphysema _____

2. Can you guess the approximate meaning of these words from Reading 1? What clues did you use?

a. chewed _____

b. Spanish conquistadors _____

c. cocaine _____

d. wonder drug _____

e. awake _____

f. dependent _____

g. poisoning _____

3. Can you guess the approximate meaning of these words from Reading 2. What clues did you use?

a. tobacco products _____

b. regularly _____

c. depressant _____

d. inhibitions _____

e. alcoholics _____

Guess Meaning from Related Words

1. The following words are in the readings. Find other words that are related to them.

Reading 1

medicine _____

benefits _____

Reading 2

addiction _____

illegal _____

2. Work in pairs. Draw a chart like this one in your notebook. Put the words from Exercise 1 in the correct columns. Compare your work with another pair when you are done.

Noun (person)	Noun (thing)	Verb	Adjective	Adverb

3. Find common words or parts of common words inside this word *long-term*.

Reading Skills

Understanding Organization

When you understand the organization of a reading, it is easier to understand and find information. There are a number of different types of organization, including the following:

a. chronological (time order)

b. comparison / contrast

c. list

d. problem / solution

Which two kinds of organization can you find in Readings 1 and 2? Each type of organization uses certain words and phrases. For example, these words and phrases show time.

- in (year)
- on (day)
- by (time)
- until (time)
- soon
- long ago
- today

Can you find some of these words and phrases in Reading 1?

Discussion

1. Which of the drugs from the readings do you think is the most dangerous? Why?

2. Are there any drugs in the readings that you think are harmless? Which ones? Why?

PART II

This reading is more difficult than the articles in Part I. Read it for the main ideas. Do not worry if you cannot understand everything.

Read the next article to find the answers to these questions.

1. What is the world's most popular drug?
2. What kinds of foods contain caffeine?
3. What does caffeine do to your brain?
4. How does caffeine make you feel?
5. What is a safe amount of caffeine?

 READING　　　　The World's Most Popular Drug

Caffeine is one of the most popular drugs in the world. It is particularly popular in the United States. Ninety percent of Americans consume it every single day. Over half consume more than 300 milligrams (mg) of caffeine every day. It is found in coffee, tea, cola, chocolate, and a variety of other things.

Most people don't know how much caffeine they take in. They also do not realize it is an addictive drug. It stimulates the brain in the same way as illegal drugs such as cocaine and heroin do. Although caffeine is not as strong as these drugs, it is still addictive. If you must have caffeine everyday, you are addicted.

Caffeine does not have the same effect on everyone. While some people can have three caffeine drinks in an hour and be fine, others may feel nervous and jumpy after just one drink. "Usually, a safe amount is no more than three eight-ounce cups, or 250 mg, a day," says one nutrition expert. She explains that when people have more caffeine than this, they start to have problems. An ounce of chocolate and the average eight-ounce soft drink both have about 25 mg of caffeine, much less than coffee.

Caffeine has some medical uses. Doctors use it as a heart stimulant. But most people take it when they feel tired and need energy. They don't realize that they are hurting themselves. When the body is tired, it needs rest.

Caffeine stops it from resting. Studies show that too much caffeine can cause nausea, anxiety, headaches, and insomnia. So when it comes to caffeine, the secret is to know what foods contain caffeine and to know your limit.

Caffeine in Common Foods
- Coffee: Coffee usually contains about 100 milligrams (mg) per six-ounce cup.
- Tea: Typical brewed tea contains 70 mg in each six-ounce cup.
- Cola drinks: Sodas contain 50 mg per 12-ounce can.
- Chocolate: Typical milk chocolate contains 6 mg per ounce.
- Common pain killers: Some aspirins contain 32 mg per tablet.
- Diet pills have about 200 mg per tablet.

Vocabulary Work

Guess Meaning from Context

What clues can you use to guess the approximate meaning of these words?

milligrams _____

consume _____

take in _____

illegal _____

jumpy _____

stimulate _____

stimulant _____

Reading Skills

Identifying Referents

What do the <u>underlined</u> pronouns and phrases refer to? Remember that sometimes pronouns do not refer to anything. Example: It is good to eat fruit. (Note: *It* has no referent. *It* refers to something outside the reading.)

1. Ninety percent of Americans consume <u>it</u> every single day.
2. Most people don't know how much caffeine <u>they</u> take in.
3. Although caffeine is not as strong as <u>these</u> drugs, it is still addictive.
4. If you must have caffeine everyday, you are addicted.
5. She explains that when people have more caffeine than <u>this</u>, . . .
6. . . . <u>they</u> start to have problems.
7. When the body is tired, <u>it</u> needs rest.
8. So when <u>it</u> comes to caffeine, the secret is to know what foods contain caffeine and to know your limit.

Idea Exchange

Think about Your Ideas

1. Which of these drugs should the government control?
    a. tobacco
    b. alcohol
    c. marijuana
    d. cocaine
    e. inhalants
    f. caffeine
    g. other   _____

2. How should they control each one?

a. Make it illegal for anyone to have it.

b. Make it illegal for anyone to sell it.

c. Make it illegal for people under 18 to have it or to sell it.

d. Tax the users.

e. Tax the companies that produce it.

f. Educate the public about it.

g. Have free treatment programs for addicts.

h. Other _____

Talk about Your Ideas

Do you agree or disagree with this statement?

Some people believe that drug use is a victimless crime. They say that drug users are only hurting themselves. Some also say that when drugs are illegal, the price of drugs goes up. As a result of this price, crime increases and hurts everyone. These people feel drugs should be legal. Do you agree?

For CNN video activities about the abuse of legal prescription drugs, turn to page 181.

CHAPTER 14

NATURE: PARADISE LOST—CAN WE GET IT BACK?

a.

b.

c.

PREVIEW

Look at these headlines. Do you believe them? Are they serious problems? Why or why not? Match each headline with a photograph above.

- **The Great Flood?—What Will Happen When the Ice in Antarctica Melts?**

- **A Way of Life Dies as the Sahara Desert Moves South**

- *Visit the Rainforest Now or You May Be Too Late*

PART I

Predict

A. Quickly skim these two articles. Circle the answers.

Which article . . .

1. talks about an island?

   Reading 1   Reading 2   Readings 1 & 2

2. discusses an environmental problem?

   Reading 1   Reading 2   Readings 1 & 2

3. says that a government caused the problem?

   Reading 1   Reading 2   Readings 1 & 2

4. discusses events in time order?

   Reading 1   Reading 2   Readings 1 & 2

B. Write a question that you think each article will answer.

Reading 1: _____

Reading 2: _____

Read It

Read the articles. Look for the answers to your questions.

 READING 1   The Story of Bikini

   After World War II, the American government wanted to test nuclear bombs. However, they had a problem. Testing nuclear bombs was dangerous; the bombs were very powerful. Furthermore, the radiation from the bombs could kill people years after the testing. Therefore, these bombs couldn't be tested near a lot of people. The government needed to find a place far away from *civilization*. They chose the tiny island of Bikini in the Pacific Ocean. Bikini seemed perfect. It was far from sea and air routes, and the U.S. government controlled it. After World War II, Bikini and the other Marshall Islands became a U.S. protectorate. Sadly, Bikini didn't get much protection.

In order to get permission to bomb, the American governor of Bikini went to talk to the people who lived on Bikini. There were only 167. He explained that the tests were for "the good of mankind and could end all world wars." He also said that the islanders could return after the tests were finished. In the end, the Bikinians agreed.

Unfortunately, nuclear scientists were wrong about the strength of the bomb. They expected it to be a five-megaton explosion, but it was a fifteen-megaton explosion. The bomb was 1,000 times stronger than the bombs that destroyed Hiroshima and Nagasaki in Japan. It caused much more dangerous radiation than they expected. Now, more than 50 years after the nuclear test, the Bikinians are still living in exile.

The nuclear testing did more than make a hole a mile wide in beautiful Bikini. It destroyed a way of life. Bikini native Emso Leviticus says that before the Americans came, "We took care of each other. No one starved." Life on Bikini was easy. Men and teenage boys went fishing every day. Then they shared the fish with everyone on the island. In the same way, when a family needed help fixing their house, everyone helped. Meanwhile, the owners of the house cooked food for the workers. Bikinian Miriam Jamodre agrees with Leviticus, "It was a pleasant life on Bikini. We all made decisions as a community of people. We made food together. It was very harmonious."

Here Today, Gone Tomorrow

Tashkent, Uzbekistan—The Aral Sea is shrinking and no one can stop it. It began getting smaller in the 1960s. At that time, the former Soviet government started a large irrigation project. They used water from the Amu Darya River and the Syr Darya River to irrigate crops. From 1960 to 1990, the area of irrigated land in Central Asia more than doubled. It increased from 3.5 million hectares to 7.5 million hectares. Cotton production also increased. Soon the region was the world's fourth largest cotton producer. Unfortunately, there were some very bad results.

With less water, the sea started to become smaller. Within decades it was 50 percent smaller. In 1989, the sea divided into two parts. Some former fishing communities are now 100 kilometers or more away from the water. However, it doesn't really matter because there are very few fish. The amount of fresh water going into the Aral is less than one-tenth of the amount in 1950. Because of this, it is now very salty. Most of the native plants and animals cannot live in such salty water. Therefore, only two kinds of fish can survive it. There used to be more than thirty kinds.

Farmers are also suffering. There is now sand where the lake used to be. The sand blows onto the farms and destroys the soil. So farmers use a lot of insecticides and fertilizers to improve soil and make their crops grow. The climate is also changing. Now, the area has shorter, hotter summers with little rain and longer, colder winters with little snow. Therefore, the growing season is shortened.

Drinking water is also a problem. The water has a lot of the insecticides and fertilizers from the farms, so it is unsafe for humans and animals. In addition, a lot of the drinking water is very salty. The salt has caused increases in kidney disease, diarrhea, and other serious health problems. In short, a place that used to be a successful farming and fishing area is now becoming an environmental wasteland.

Reading Comprehension

Check Your Predictions

1. Look back at questions 1–4 in the Predict section. How correct were your predictions?

Prediction	Correct	Incorrect
1		
2		
3		
4		

2. If you found the answers to your questions, what were they?

   Reading 1: _____

   Reading 2: _____

Check the Facts

(READING 1)

A. Read the statements and write _true_ (T) or _false_ (F). Go back to Reading 1 and look for the answers you are unsure of.

_____ 1. Bikini is an island in the Atlantic Ocean.

_____ 2. A lot of people used to live on Bikini.

_____ 3. The United States controls Bikini.

_____ 4. The bomb was stronger than scientists expected it to be.

_____ 5. No one lives on Bikini today.

B. Answer the questions.

1. Why are nuclear bombs more dangerous than other bombs?

   _____

   _____

2. How did the U.S. government persuade the Bikinians to agree to the testing?

   _____

   _____

READING 2

A. Read the statements and write *true* (T) or *false* (F). Go back to Reading 2 and look for the answers you are unsure of.

_____ 1. The Aral Sea had salt water.

_____ 2. The government used a lot of the river water for farms.

_____ 3. At first, the irrigated farms grew fewer crops than before.

_____ 4. The main crop in the area is rice.

_____ 5. Some fishing villages are no longer on the sea.

_____ 6. There are no fish in the sea.

B. Answer the questions.

1. How is the Aral Sea different today from 50 years ago?

   _____

   _____

   _____

2. How are the lives of the farmers and fisherman in the area different than they were 30 years ago?

   _____

   _____

   _____

Analyze

Compare the story of Bikini and the Aral Sea.

1. Why did each problem happen?

2. Did the governments understand the consequences of their actions?

3. Which situation is more important? Why do you think so?

Vocabulary Work

Guess Meaning from Context

1. Use *world knowledge* to help you understand the following words and phrases.

Reading 1	Reading 2
nuclear bomb	irrigation
radiation	fresh water
five-megaton	crops
explosion	hectares
	fertilizer
	insecticide

2. What clues can help you guess the approximate meaning of the following words and phrases?

in exile	shrinking	sand
starved	consequences	climate
harmonious	survive	diarrhea

Guess Meaning from Related Words

1. The following words are in the readings. Find other words that are related to them.

Reading 1

Bikini _____

protection _____

stronger _____

Reading 2

irrigate _____ _____

salt _____

2. Work in pairs. Draw a chart like this one in your notebook. Put the words from Exercise 1 in the correct columns. Compare your work with another pair when you are done.

Noun (person)	Noun (place, thing)	Verb	Adjective	Adverb

Reading Skills

Identifying Transition Words and Phrases

1. Reading 1 contains many transition words and phrases. Find each word in the box in the reading. Look how it is used. Write it on the correct line below.

however	therefore	after	sadly	in the end
unfortunately	now	then	in the same way	meanwhile

a. To introduce an opposite idea _____

b. To introduce a result _____

c. To introduce a cause _____

d. To mark time _____

e. To give the author's opinion _____

f. To show how similarity _____

2. Find four transition words and phrases in Reading 2 that mark time.

_____

_____

_____

_____

Analyzing the Organization of a Reading

Reading 2 is a long series of causes and results. As a reader, you must be able to understand this order. Complete the following chart of causes and results.

CAUSE: Water from rivers used to irrigate crops

RESULT: Region becomes world's fourth largest cotton producer

RESULT: Aral Sea becomes smaller

RESULT: Some fishing communities now far from sea

RESULT: Very few _____

RESULT: Sea is very _____

RESULT: Most of the native plants and animals

_____

RESULT: Land is now sandy.

RESULT: Farmers use a lot of _____

_____

RESULT: _____ changing because of the sand.

RESULT: _____

RESULT: Water is a problem.

RESULT: Water has insecticides and fertilizers

RESULT: _____

RESULT: Drinking water is salty

RESULT: _____

Discussion

1. Should governments be responsible for fixing the environmental problems they cause? Why or why not?

2. Do governments today make these same kinds of mistakes? Why or why not?

PART II

This reading is more difficult than the articles in Part I. Read it for the main ideas. Do not worry if you cannot understand everything.

Read to find the answers to these questions.

1. What is Nauru and where is it?
2. How was life on Nauru 200 years ago?
3. What did people discover on Nauru?
4. What is strip mining?
5. How was life on Nauru 20 years ago?
6. How is life on Nauru today?

 (**READING**)   # The Three Naurus

The Pacific island nation of Nauru is one of the loneliest and saddest countries in the world. It used to be a beautiful place. Then, for a short while, it was a very rich place. Now it is an ecological nightmare. Nauru's heartbreaking story could have one good consequence—other countries might learn from its mistakes.

Pleasant Island

For thousands of years, Polynesian people lived on the remote island of Nauru, far from western civilization. The first European to arrive was John Fearn in 1798. He was the British captain of the *Hunter*, a whaling ship. He described the island as very attractive. Everywhere there were small houses that belonged to the twelve clans or family groups of the island. He called the island *Pleasant Island*.

However, because it was very remote, Nauru had little communication with Europeans at first. Then whaling ships and other traders began to visit. They brought guns and alcohol. These elements destroyed the social balance of the twelve tribes. A ten-year civil war started. It reduced the population from 1,400 to 900. Finally, in 1888, Germany took Nauru as a protectorate.

Fantasy Island

Nauru's real troubles began in 1899. In that year, a British mining company discovered phosphate on the island. In fact, it found that the island of Nauru was nearly all phosphate. Phosphate is a very important fertilizer and farming was an important industry. The company began mining the phosphate.

A phosphate mine is not a hole in the ground; it is a strip mine. When a company strip-mines, it removes the top layer of soil. Then it takes away the material it wants. Strip-mining totally destroys the land. Gradually, the lovely island of Nauru started to look like the moon.

In 1968, Nauru received its independence. It became the smallest republic in the world. It was also one of the richest. Every year the government received millions and millions of dollars for its phosphate.

Desert Island

Unfortunately, the government did not use this money well. The leaders invested unwisely and lost millions of dollars. In addition, they used millions more dollars for personal expenses. Soon people realized that they

(Continued on next page.)

Ninety percent of Nauru looks like this.

had a terrible problem. Their phosphate was running out. Ninety percent of their island was destroyed and they had nothing. By 2000, Nauru was almost bankrupt. Experts say that it would take approximately $433,600,000 and more than 20 years to repair the island. This will probably never happen. The only people who want to do it are the Naurans and they have nothing.

Vocabulary Work

Guess Words from Context

What clues can help you guess the approximate meaning of the words and phrases below. Discuss.

ecological nightmare

heartbreaking

remote

whaling ship

clans

alcohol

reduced

strip-mining

running out

bankrupt

unwisely

Reading Skills

Identifying Transition Words and Phrases

Find nine transition words and phrases that the writer uses to mark time. Find two he uses to add an idea. Find one he uses to emphasize an idea.

Mark Time	Add Ideas	Emphasize an Idea
_____	_____	_____
_____	_____	_____
_____	_____	_____
_____	_____	_____

Idea Exchange

Think about Your Ideas

1. How big a problem is the environment today? Explain.

2. Are each of the groups below responsible for environmental problems? Why or why not?

   a. ordinary citizens in developed countries

   b. leaders of corporations

   c. officials in governments

   d. scientists such as geologists

   e. ordinary citizens in developing countries

3. How can each group help to solve these environmental problems?

Talk about Your Ideas

Work in groups.

1. Name the three biggest ecological problems we have today.

   _____

   _____

   _____

2. In your opinion, what is the cause or causes of each problem?

   _____

   _____

   _____

3. What are possible solutions to each problem?

   _____

   _____

   _____

4. What are possible obstacles to these solutions?

   _____

   _____

   _____

For CNN video activities about other environmental problems, turn to page 182.

APPENDIX: CNN Video Activities

CHAPTER 1 Pampering Your Pet

Think about It

Before you watch the video, think about these questions.

1. What do you do with your pets when you go away? Where do they stay?
2. What kinds of treats do you give your pets?
3. Do you know celebrities that have pets? What are their names? What kinds of pets do they have?

Understand It

Read the questions below. Then watch the video once or twice. As you watch the video, listen for the answers to these questions. Check (✓) the correct answers.

1. What kind of treats do owners buy for their dogs?
   _____ a. fish   _____ c. sushi
   _____ b. biscuits   _____ d. chocolate
2. How much is a room with a TV at the cat hotel?
   _____ a. $45   _____ c. $25
   _____ b. $35   _____ d. $15
3 What kind of surgery is popular for animals?
   _____ a. orthopedic   _____ c. obstetrical
   _____ b. cosmetic   _____ d. oral
4. Which alternative therapy does one doctor use to compliment western therapies?
   _____ a. hypnosis   _____ c. music
   _____ b. massage   _____ d. acupuncture

Discuss It

1. Do you think people should spend so much money on pets? Why or why not?
2. Talk about your favorite pet.

Write about It

Make a questionnaire to survey people with pets. Ask questions about food, treats, medical care, and about what they do with their pets when they go on vacation. Tell the class your results.

CHAPTER 2 The Sport of Eating

Think about It

Before you watch the video, think about these questions.

1. What is your opinion of eating competitions?
2. Are there eating contests in other countries besides the United States?

Understand It

A. Read the questions. Then watch the video once or twice. As you watch the video, listen for the answers to these questions. Check (✓) the correct answers.

1. How many minutes do the competitors have to eat the Thanksgiving dinner?

   _____ a. 8 minutes   _____ c. 12 minutes

   _____ b. 10 minutes   _____ d. 15 minutes

2. How much does each plate weigh?

   _____ a. ½ pound   _____ c. 1½ pounds

   _____ b. 1 pound   _____ d. 2 pounds

3. The competitors may not _____ their food.

   _____ a. eat   _____ c. show

   _____ b. consume   _____ d. shovel

4. How many plates did the winner eat?

   _____ a. 4   _____ c. 5

   _____ b. 4½   _____ d. 5½

B. Match the champions to the eating competitions.

_____ 1. Dale Boone   a. jalapeno peppers

_____ 2. George Lerman   b. donuts

_____ 3. Eric Booker   c. reindeer

Discuss It

1. Do you think eating contests are a good thing or a bad thing? Why?
2. Do you participate in eating contests? What can you eat a lot of quickly?

Write about It

Make a poster advertising a local eating competition. Include information on food, rules, and prizes.

CHAPTER 3 State-sponsored Marriage in Oklahoma

Think about It

Before you watch the video, think about these questions.

1. Do you think divorce is a cause of poverty or poverty is a cause of divorce?
2. In your experience, which families with children have more financial problems: married, divorced, or never married?

Understand It

Read the statements below. Then watch the video once or twice. Listen for the words that complete these sentences and fill in the blanks.

five	workshops	marry	divorce
poor	initiative	experiment	tax payers

1. Oklahoma has the second highest _____ rate in the country.
2. The governor has launched a marriage _____.
3. The poverty rate for single mothers is _____ times that of married couples.
4. _____ people are less likely to get married and less likely to stay married.
5. Some money goes to training volunteers to run marriage _____.
6. Eight hundred ministers in Oklahoma will only _____ couples who go through counseling first.
7. _____ pay the price when marriage falls apart in welfare, broken homes, and damaged children.
8. Governor Keating admits the marriage initiative is an _____.

Discuss It

1. Homes without fathers account for
   - over 60 percent of youth suicides
   - the majority of homeless / runaway children
   - the majority of children with behavior problems
   - the majority of high school dropouts
   - the majority of youths in prison
   - more than half of teen mothers (Source: www.divorcemag.com)
   Discuss and think of reasons why this may be true.
2. Do you think the marriage initiative in Oklahoma is going to be successful?

Write about It

Your son or daughter is going to get married. Write a letter giving some advice.

CHAPTER 4 'TWEEN ADDICTION TO SHOPPING

Think about It

Before you watch the video, think about the following questions.

1. Do you have healthy or unhealthy financial habits? Explain.
2. Did anyone teach you about saving and spending when you were a child?
3. Do children you know have healthy or unhealthy financial habits?

Understand It

A. Read the statements. Then watch the video once or twice. According to the video, which statements are true and which statements are false? Write *T* for *true* or *F* for *false*.

_____ 1. Rosie saves her money.

_____ 2. Rosie's mother is trying to teach her about money management.

_____ 3. Tweens don't spend a lot of money.

_____ 4. Some children take courses in financial awareness.

_____ 5. Nathan Dungan says parents should teach children "Share, save, spend."

_____ 6. Rosie's mother is going to give up on Rosie.

B. According to Nathan Dungan, what does "share, save, spend" teach children? Match Column A with Column B.

Column A	Column B
_____ 1. share	a. the difference between needs and wants
_____ 2. save	b. sensitivity and gratitude
_____ 3. spend	c. patience and discipline

Discuss It

1. What do you think about "Share, save, and spend"?
2. Do you think financial awareness classes for kids are a good idea?
3. *If you had bad financial habits as a child, you'll probably have bad financial habits as an adult.* Do you agree or disagree with this statement?

Write about It

Write a list of ten ways to save money. Share your ideas.

CHAPTER 5 — *The Gambling Lifestyle*

Think about It

Before you watch the video, think about the following questions.

1. Do you like to go to casinos? How often do you go?
2. Describe the typical gambler. Is it a man or woman? Young or old? Rich or poor? Educated or uneducated?

Understand it

Before you watch the video, read the statements. Watch the video once or twice. As you watch the video, listen for the words that complete these sentences. Write the words from the box in the blanks.

coupon	woman	attend
income	groceries	twenty-six

1. Each year 50 million Americans lose _____ billion dollars at casinos.
2. We spend more money each year on gambling than we do on _____.
3. The typical casino gambler is a middle-aged _____.
4. Her household _____ is about $50,000.
5. Fifty-six percent are _____ clippers.
6. Gamblers are 11 percent less likely to _____ a place of worship than non-gamblers.

Discuss It

1. Did the description of a typical casino gambler surprise you? Why or why not?
2. Do you think gambling can be an addiction? Why or why not?

Write about It

Think about the characteristics of the typical casino gambler. Make an advertisement for a casino to attract this kind of gambler.

CHAPTER 6 Actress Nabbed in Shoplifting Scandal

Think about It

Before you watch the video, think about these questions.

1. What is the penalty for shoplifting in your community?
2. How many people in your class know who Winona Ryder is? What did she do? Where did she do it? What happened to her?

Understand It

Read the statements. Then watch the video once or twice. Choose the correct answer.

1. Winona Ryder was found guilty of _____.
   a. fraud
   b. vandalism
   c. robbery
   d. commercial burglary
2. The jury was shown a surveillance _____ of most of Ryder's movements.
   a. tape
   b. camera
   c. photo
   d. report
3. The security manager saw Ryder stuffing items into _____.
   a. a bag
   b. her coat
   c. her shoes
   d. a hat
4. One employee saw Ryder cutting _____ from merchandise.
   a. tags
   b. sleeves
   c. buttons
   d. bags
5. Ryder said she was _____ for a movie about a shoplifter.
   a. writing the script
   b. buying clothes
   c. observing people
   d. doing research.
6. Ryder has to _____ for her conduct.
   a. go to jail
   b. run away
   c. take responsibility
   d. make money

Discuss It

Discuss Winona Ryder's punishment: Complete 480 hours of community service, pay more than $10,000 in fines, and undergo drug and psychological counseling. Do you think the sentence or punishment was fair?

Write about It

With a partner, write a short skit about shoplifting.

CHAPTER 7 OBESITY: NOT SIMPLY AN AMERICAN PROBLEM

Think about It

Before you watch the video, think about these questions.

1. Watch the first 20 seconds of video without any sound. What city or country do you think these people are from?
2. Do you think there is an obesity problem in other countries?

Understand It

Read the statements. Then watch the video once or twice. Match the sentences based on the information from the video.

_____ 1. Obesity is becoming
_____ 2. The problem in the Middle East is just as
_____ 3. Average life expectancy in obese people
_____ 4. The life expectancy of obese children
_____ 5. Fatty foods and lack of exercise

a. is reduced by almost nine years.
b. cause obesity
c. will be less than their parents or grandparents.
d. the most serious health problem in the world.
e. bad as the problem in the United States.

Discuss It

1. Do you agree that healthy and thin people are paying for the obesity problem? Why or why not?
2. Why do you think many countries, not just the U.S., have problems with obesity?

Write about It

Write down everything you eat for one week. Are you a healthy eater? Compare with a partner.

CHAPTER 8   Fortune or Fraud? The Truth about Business Opportunity

Think about It

Before you watch the video, think about these questions.

1. Where are "get-rich-quick" scams advertised?
2. Name some "get-rich-quick" scams that you know about.

Understand It

Read the statements. Then watch the video once or twice. What are some main ideas from the video? Check (✓) all that apply.

_____ 1. Jeffrey bought vending machines as an investment.
_____ 2. Vending machines are an interesting business.
_____ 3. Jeffrey researched the company and called references.
_____ 4. Every year, many people stop working and retire.
_____ 5. Jeffrey earned a lot of money on the machines.
_____ 6. Many companies deceive investors about big profits.
_____ 7. The Federal Trade Commission (FTC) is cracking down on deceptive businesses.

Discuss It

1. A get-rich-quick scam is fraud. What other kinds of fraud are there?
2. How can we recognize fraud? Together, make a list of ways to recognize it.

Write about It

Go through newspapers and magazines and watch advertisements on TV. Write down all the names of ads you think may be scams or fraudulent.

CHAPTER 9 RACING TOWARD STARDOM— OR SCANDAL?

Think about It

Before you watch the video, think about these questions.

1. If you saw an athlete taking a drug to improve his or her performance, would you report the incident? Why or why not?
2. Do you know who Trevor Graham is? What is his connection to sport and to sports doping? Do you know any other athletes involved with drugs?

Understand it

Before you watch the video, read the statements. Watch the video once or twice. As you watch the video, listen for the words that complete these sentences. Write the words from the box in the blanks.

nice	coached	banned
use	sent	coach

1. Trevor Graham _____ Marion Jones in the Sydney Olympics.
2. Graham _____ a syringe with THG to sports officials.
3. Graham is Justin Gatlin's _____.
4. Gaitlin wanted to show everyone that _____ guys can finish first.
5. At the Athens's Olympics, six athletes tested positive for _____ substances.
6. Now athletes won't _____ THG.

Discuss It

1. A sports official in the video said that cheaters are only one step ahead. Do you think it's possible to get rid of drug use in sports?
2. How do you feel about the Olympics now that there are so many problems with doping?

Write about It

Make a poster to educate young athletes about sports doping.

CHAPTER 10 WHITE-COLLAR CRIME: IS IT WORTH IT?

Think about It

Before you watch the video, think about and discuss these questions.

1. Can you name any famous people who are white-collar criminals?
2. What percentage of white-collar crimes do you think get prosecuted each year? What percentage of drug crimes do you think get prosecuted each year?

Understand It

Read the statements. Then watch the video once or twice. Answer the questions based on the information in the video.

1. What percentage of white-collar crimes gets prosecuted each year?

   _____

2. What percentage of white-collar criminals goes to prison each year?

   _____

3. What percentage of drug crimes gets prosecuted each year?

   _____

4. What percentage of drug criminals go to prison each year?

   _____

5. How long was Steve Madden in jail for fraud?

   _____

6. What is the *number one* deterrent to white-collar crime?

   _____

Discuss It

1. Do you think cheating on a test or copying someone else's work is a type of white-collar crime? Why or why not?
2. Do you think cheating and copying in school create habits that may lead to serious white-collar crimes in the future?

Write about It

Write a letter to a representative in Congress about getting tough on white-collar crimes. Include statistics you learned from the video.

(CHAPTER 11) *HOMELESS AT CHRISTMAS: ONE FAMILY'S STORY*

Think about It

Before you watch the video, think about these questions.

1. Do you know anyone that is or has been homeless? What's their story?
2. Have you ever been to a homeless shelter or a soup kitchen? What did you think about the people you met there?

Understand It

Read the statements. Then watch the video once or twice. According to the video, which statements are true and which statements are false? Write *T* for *true* or *F* for *false*.

_____ 1. Tamikio has lived in the shelter with her kids for seven months.

_____ 2. A small percentage of homeless are families.

_____ 3. Homeless children don't often do well in school.

_____ 4. Shelters don't get many donations during Christmas.

_____ 5. The number of homeless families is decreasing.

_____ 6. About 40 percent of requests for shelter were from families with children.

Discuss It

1. How much is the minimum wage in your city? How much is the rent for an apartment? Discuss other typical monthly expenses.
2. Do you think it may be easy to become homeless in your town or city? Why or why not?

Write about It

How can homeless shelters help families "get back on their feet"? Write down some ideas.

CHAPTER 12 Child Beauty Pageants: Fulfilling Dreams?

Think about It

Before you watch the video, think about the following questions.

1. How do you feel about child beauty pageants?
2. Would you enter your child in a beauty contest?

Understand It

Before you watch the video, read the statements. Watch the video once or twice. As you watch the video, listen for the words that complete these sentences. Write the words from the box in the blanks.

life	self-esteem	dream	3,000
overdo	100,000	inappropriate	makeup

1. More than _____ children a year under 12 participate in beauty pageants.

2. There are about _____ child pageants a year in the United States.

3. People who like child pageants say they are cute slices of American _____.

4. Critics say that pageants are _____.

5. Some say that pageants improve children's _____.

6. Pageant organizers admit that sometimes parents _____ it.

7. Sometimes children wear too much _____.

8. Some girls _____ about being Miss America.

Discuss It

1. Talk about positive and negative aspects of child beauty pageants. Make a list.

2. Why aren't there beauty pageants for young boys in the United States?

Write about It

How can you make child beauty pageants better? Write up a list of rules that could make a child beauty pageant a safe and healthy experience for children.